Praise for **CHERYL ECTON** and *Choices Change EVERYTHING*

"Cheryl's story will definitely impact your life! Her resilience, strength and courage to succeed are core fibers of her life. This amazing book is a first-hand account of how adversity and challenges can be positively impactful. I highly recommend this book, as it allows you to understand how to overcome obstacles and disappointments on your path to success. Cheryl's story allows the reader to foresee the success that they were meant to achieve."

—Albert Dileonardo CEO, Cutco/Vector

ଔ

"The timing for Cheryl's book to come out couldn't be better! The pressures on women managing life, family, and career have never been greater. Cheryl has the ability to inspire her readers to press on and never give up! Truly an inspiration!"

—Joan Winchester, President /CEO,
Franchise Advise, LLC

"A compelling and awe-inspiring read! Cheryl's journey resonates with many of us who have faced obstacles and adversity in life. Through her refreshing and authentic story, spoken from the heart, Cheryl defines the path she took and how, by grit, determination, tenacity, and perseverance, emboldens her readers to believe in themselves and triumph over life's challenges to create the life they deserve and can achieve."

—Catherine Allen-Carlozo, CFP®, HFM Investment Advisors, LLC

℗

"Everyone that has had challenges in life can relate to Cheryl's story. Often it is tough to see the steps we can take to turn those challenges into the lessons we need to move forward and become better versions of ourselves. This is what reading Cheryl's story offers. If you are looking for practical takeaways as well as inspiration to level up, this book is for you. I highly recommend this personal first-hand account for its universal appeal."

—Jennifer Lynn Robinson, Esquire, CEO, Purposeful Networking

Choices Change EVERYTHING

Choose to Get Up
When Life Knocks You Down

CHERYL ECTON

Published by:
Hailyn Enterprises
WILMINGTON, DE

Copyright © 2022 Cheryl Ecton

ISBN-13s:
979-8-9856872-0-0 (Print)
979-8-9856872-1-7 (Epub)

Editorial consultation
Natalie Silver and Bill Tonelli

Cover and interior
Gary A. Rosenberg • www.thebookcouple.com

Front cover photo
Laura Eaton Photography

Printed in the United States of America

*To the millions of women who have
struggled with work-life balance
and managed to stay focused, strong and
fearless to meet their goals and dreams.*

Contents

Introduction

I always say that life is not a ladder, it's a lattice. I think this is especially true for women.

At a young age, we're handed this image of success being like climbing a ladder. All we need to do, we're told, is rise up, one step after another, and we'll go from the bottom to the top (or as close as we're ever going to get).

I bought into it. Maybe you did, too. Just don't get distracted, don't get sidetracked, don't slow down, keep on climbing, and you'll get there. One step at a time. Sounds simple.

Well, my life has definitely not been like a ladder. It's been more like a lattice. I have encountered a few rungs leading upward, but quite a few more that went sideways. There were obstacles that got in my way and slowed me down. Some broken steps. More detours than I expected.

If I were still looking for that ladder, I'd be

discouraged by now. Maybe even tempted to quit climbing. Instead, I feel comforted when I realize that every obstacle I've faced has just sent me in a new direction forward. The goal isn't always *up*. The path isn't truly straight. It sometimes goes zigzag. Once in a while, it moves backward. Sometimes, no path is visible, and you'll wonder if one even exists.

Eventually, I know, I'll reach my destination, but there will be some unanticipated twists and turns along the way. Some may be positive, even helpful, but not all.

I'll deal with it. I'll make it work.

I feel as though I'm now in a position to speak to others about ladders and lattices. My lattice has quite a bit of dirt on it, which I'll explain. But there are beautiful flowers growing on it, too, and I'll talk about that as well.

I hear from many women who feel left behind if they can't devote 100 percent of their time and energies to their careers. They're mothers and wives, with families who depend on them. They don't have nannies and cooks and housekeepers, or personal assistants to handle life's normal responsibilities for them. These women have to juggle everything themselves. And they don't have MBAs from Ivy

League universities or other lofty stops on their resumes. They've heard all the voices telling women they need to "lean in." But not all of us are in a position to lean in. Lots of us don't even really *want* to lean in.

I know what that feels like. I only have a high school diploma. I had to build a business while taking care of a daughter with serious medical complications, as well as a husband and a young son. My idea of who I am is more traditional and conventional than lots of business self-help books would advise.

Did my life choices hold me back? I don't think so. You have to be yourself and live your own life. None of that will get in your way if you don't let it. I still don't know exactly what "lean in" means. But our destinies aren't guaranteed no matter which way we lean.

Seeing life as a lattice allows you to exist and improve without always being focused on achieving the next big leap forward. You can actually live your life, and even enjoy it, when you're not constantly focused only on moving straight up. You can get off that rigid path and slow down when life is telling you to, like when you're raising young children, or caring for a sick parent, or dealing with issues in your marriage. You don't need to always be worried that you aren't rising up fast enough, or keeping up with the competition. Finding contentment is also part of a successful and happy life. Becoming the person you always wanted to be—the *whole* person—is an important goal, too. Do what you want to do and what you need to do. You'll find your way.

I know I did.

CHAPTER 1

I Can Do This

"Jerry, I'd like to make you a proposal."

I stand at the threshold of my boss's office, waiting for him to reply. I am nervous yet determined. I remind myself that I've been rehearsing this conversation over and over for several days.

"Cheryl, come in."

Jerry and his business partner, Bill, own a financial services firm. They hired me for a secretarial job. Jerry was the nice boss. That's why I'm approaching him first.

He motions me into his big corner office without looking up from his work. I try to find a comfortable spot in front of his desk. Do I sit or stand? My hands start to sweat, and I can feel my throat tighten. But I am going to say my piece. I inch up closer to his desk, careful not to roll an ankle or trip in my high heels. I need to exude confidence right now. I can't come across as a nervous young newlywed, pregnant to boot, with only a high school diploma. Although that's what I am.

My new husband and I had just moved back home to Wilmington, Delaware, from Baltimore. We were living paycheck to paycheck, with not a dollar extra to spend. My in-laws had to give us the down payment on our little house, and we could only afford furniture for two rooms.

Jerry and Bill have been my bosses for the past year. I answer phones, open email, manage their schedules, and keep the office orderly. I often find myself taking calls from tenants in our building, which Jerry and Bill own.

I finally decide to sit in the chair in front of Jerry's desk. He looks up and folds his hands. My moment has arrived. I begin my prepared speech.

"Jerry, all day long I get calls from your tenants complaining about the cleaning company. They miss important details, or they don't show up at all. Someone said the same paperclip has been on their floor for over a week, and another tenant says it's been days since the trash was emptied. And have you noticed that the lobby is starting to look pretty dingy? I know I can do a better job than your current cleaning company. I saw what they charge after I opened their invoice the other day. Pay me what you pay them and you'll never have any complaints. I promise that it won't interfere with my work here during the day. So, will you hire me to clean the building?"

Wow. I finished the speech and delivered all the points I wanted to make. *How did I just do that?*

Jerry looks at me closely. He pauses for a moment, which makes me even more nervous. Was this idea totally crazy? Was I completely out of line just for asking?

"Cheryl," he says, "if you think you can do this without it interfering with your work here, I guess you're making me an offer I can't pass up. Go ahead."

And just like that, I now have two jobs.

My adrenaline is pumping when I leave Jerry's office. It's not only from the thought that I'll be earning more money. It's because my first-ever sales pitch was successful. This is the first time in my adult life that I feel powerful. In control. I went after something and I got it!

But then I wonder, do I really want to work all day and then clean offices at night?

The short answer is yes. My husband and I are thrilled to be starting a family of our own, but money is tight. He has a job, and I was fortunate to find work with Jerry and Bill, though it doesn't pay much. We are still kids—I'm just twenty-one and he's twenty-six—and we haven't had time to accumulate savings. Once the baby arrives, our budget will be even tighter than it is now.

But there's another reason I'm glad: My pitch to Jerry is the first time I've ever had anything like a professional life—like the beginnings of a career. I've only been out of high school for a few years and got married almost immediately after. We were in love and wanted the security that comes with marriage before we moved away from our hometown for his job.

I guess you'd call me a child bride, considering that my parents had to sign for me on our wedding day—but I was only two months shy of eighteen! Despite our youth, we knew we wanted to be together. We'd met as little kids, and then reconnected when I was in high school. Though he was working on the West Coast by then and I was 3,000 miles away, in Delaware, we talked on the phone constantly and exchanged plenty of love notes.

During my senior year he decided to move back East, and his cross-country relocation made it official. I was so in love with him and our life together that I didn't exactly ask myself what I wanted to be when I grew up.

Despite not enrolling in college or thinking beyond a weekly paycheck, I felt confident that I'd find success at something. When I was a child I wanted to be a doctor someday. Clearly, that wasn't going to happen. But I didn't feel hopeless. Cleaning offices at night wasn't my dream occupation, for sure. But I got a definite rush when Jerry said he'd accept my proposal.

That moment reminded me of my strengths. When faced with a challenge, I could rise to the occasion and outwardly present self-confidence. This quality was crucial once I took the big leap and started working for myself. I think back to my days as a cheerleader. I had to come across as friendly and—dare I say—cheerful on the sidelines of basketball games. It didn't matter if I was having a bad day, or stressed about an upcoming test, or arguing with a friend. When I was cheering, I had to be on and sell it. Even if we were getting beat to shreds or were performing away from home, I had to manage the task at hand: to cheer my team to victory. I had to wave my pom-poms, clap my hands, form a pyramid, and shout chants in my happiest, loudest voice. People make fun of cheerleaders, but so many of the skills and attitudes I learned back then prepared me for future sales pitches.

Even before that, my parents got me started right. We moved around a bit, from Florida to California to Pennsylvania, but my siblings and I always felt connected and happy. Our parents had their own goals and gave 100 percent to achieve them. This didn't just apply to their professional lives. They instilled the drive for hard work and good values throughout our childhoods. They enjoyed the fun of life, too. We took great vacations that helped us grow together as a family. I think that's why I yearned to live near them when I was ready to have children of my own.

My parents' keen insights into raising children became apparent as I finished high school. I was a smart kid, but I started to stray from academics once boys came into the picture. Even when dating and hanging out with friends took over as my top interests, my folks never lost faith in me. They still encouraged me to keep up cheerleading, study hard, and follow my own path no matter where it led. This became obvious when they allowed me to get married despite being underage, and watched without complaint as I moved away from home, still a teenager, with my new husband.

Still, the sense of who I could someday become wasn't always apparent to me back then. At twenty, I had no visions of a professional life. I wanted only to support my husband in his career, and maybe find a job so we could pay our bills and have a little fun, too. Being a receptionist was dull, but it suited me fine. In the beginning, I didn't mind coming into work and doing my job.

As time went on, however, I began to realize I wanted more out of life—more than taking messages and ordering supplies, more than just scraping by financially. Recognizing the need for a better cleaning service in the building, and then pitching myself as the solution, was the first time I thought that I might enjoy having a business of my own.

But to make that happen, first I had to roll my sleeves up and clean.

4:59 PM

The second hand rounds its way around the clock face one last time. I've already worked a full day at the office with Jerry and Bill. I begin to close down my cubicle, rummaging through paperwork a final time and scribbling notes about what to remember tomorrow. Then I pull the gym bag out from under my desk, say goodnight to everyone, and head to the bathroom—to change into my office-cleaning clothes. It's time for my second workday to begin.

I have two looks at work. One is the polished young secretary look—tailored blouses, skirts, and jackets; nylons and high heels; styled hair with plenty of hairspray and feathering; and grown-up makeup. At five, I change into jeans or sweatpants and an oversized T-shirt to cover my ever-growing pregnant body. My hair goes back into a ponytail. I lace up my sneakers and prepare for a four- or five-hour night shift.

Cleaning this place is work. It's a four-story building in downtown Wilmington with several tenants. I tackle one office at a time, dusting, vacuuming, and emptying the trashcans. Then I move to the kitchens and bathrooms. And, yes, there are plenty of toilets to scrub. On certain weeks, I do deep cleaning, like wiping baseboards and polishing light fixtures. I try to keep my cleanliness standards high despite how exhausting it is to manage this alone night after night while seven, eight, nine months pregnant. I don't want anything to ruin my reputation as a hard worker—even if I'm practically ready to give birth to my baby, and my back and legs ache from carrying around these extra pounds.

While the days and nights are long, I really enjoy this second job. I don't think I want to clean offices forever, but I always get a strong sense of satisfaction when I receive the monthly check for my services. This job has allowed my husband and me to put away a little money, which couldn't have come at a better time.

But with the baby's arrival imminent, I need to figure out where I want to go with my professional life. I'd like to keep cleaning the building after our child arrives. Once I get into the groove, the job feels like easy money. I listen to music on my Walkman and shuffle around with my duster and vacuum while the hours fly. I like that I can control the pace and take charge without having anyone supervise me. I work hard and get the paydays to prove it.

So I am determined to work both jobs. Thankfully, my pregnancy goes well. I am able to maintain the pace right up until I deliver my son. Ryan is born in June, three weeks early but with no complications. He arrives on a day that gives him a rather special birthday—6/7/89. I have a little money saved to take maternity leave, though I can't stay out for long. My husband and I both have family nearby who can help. I line up a friend to watch Ryan during the day.

Having a child is overwhelming and joyous all at once. My husband and I, barely out of childhood ourselves, are quickly immersed in the chaos of sleeping, feeding, and caring for a newborn. Despite having mommy brain, I feel more determined than ever to keep my company afloat and maybe even grow it. But I'm less excited to return to my receptionist job.

Just a few months after Ryan's birth, I head back to work—receptionist by day, janitor by night. Except now the schedule isn't so easy to maintain. I'm feeling stretched way too thin. Bill and Jerry are good bosses, but I'm not in a position to ask for flexibility in my day job since I promised I wouldn't let the cleaning get in the way.

But it's obvious that something's going to give. I feel overwhelmed every single day. I wake up early in the morning, work eight hours as a receptionist, and then change clothes to clean the building. I get home around 10, and then, often, I type my husband's real estate appraisal reports until midnight.

Even with Ryan to care for, I stick to the same routine. I rush home from the office, feed the baby, bathe him, and tuck him into bed. Then I race back out into the night and clean offices for several hours. And then return home to do my husband's typing. I am exhausted all the time, and still I feel guilty—about being a bad mom, a bad wife, about choosing to work so many hours.

As dusk rolls in each evening and I begin cleaning offices, the wheels in my head start to spin. I sweep floors and dust blinds and wonder: *Do I really want to quit my day job and clean even more buildings? If not, can we make it just on my income from cleaning Bill and Jerry's building? But how will I grow my business if that's what I want to do? Do I need to hire employees?*

One night while cleaning, my emotions overwhelm me: I finally accept the fact that I'm trying to do more than I can manage, and not succeeding at anything. I yearn for more time with my son and husband. But I also want enough money to live a nicer life. And I'm tired of packing my cleaning clothes every morning as I head out the door dressed in receptionist garb. I'm trying to be two people. I can't do it. I need a change.

And that's when I realize it's time to make a move. It's going to be bold. It's going to take courage. Despite my reservations and even some doubts, I tell myself: *You can do this.*

CHERYL'S TIP FOR SUCCESS:
Start Small

Even after I landed my first client, I didn't know I would become an entrepreneur. But I did know that I had something to sell that could compete against what anyone else was selling. This was when I realized that I could actually make a business of this. Here is a tip to consider when starting a company: Don't plan to build an empire overnight. At the beginning, I identified a single service I could provide in a thorough and consistent way: I could clean. That was all I needed. For months, I had just one client. This helped me focus on what I needed to do if my business was going to get bigger.

CHAPTER 2

It's Time to Move Forward

Ryan is six months old when I give Jerry and Bill my notice. I want to keep cleaning your building at night, I tell them. But I need to quit my day job. I thank them for their confidence in me and for being my first client. But if I'm going to grow my cleaning business and make something of it, it needs my full attention.

Even with all that, I feel guilty. I was only able to start a business because they allowed me to clean their offices at a time when I really needed the extra money. And now, here I was, quitting. They would easily find somebody to replace me in the office, I knew. Still, it felt like I was abandoning them.

But I had bigger things to worry about. With the loss of income from my receptionist job, I definitely need to ramp up my marketing efforts for the cleaning gig. The first thing I have to do is name the company. I want something that gets attention. I need something that describes what we're about and what I bring to the table. I begin to scour the Yellow Pages and realize something important: I should choose a name that puts me near the top of the alphabetical listings. For some reason, the letter E pops into my head, which will put me close to the top. What starts with E? Excellent and exceptional cross my mind, but they don't feel quite right.

And then the magic, meant-to-be word pops into my head: Elite.

That describes the level of service I want my company to provide. It says that we're in a class of our own, offering services beyond any of our competition. Once I decide on the name, I get really excited. I can visualize growing this company and brand. It's time to hit the streets.

In the 1980s, pre–social media, it's hard to get your name out into the world. Physical work is involved. I can't rely on mailings or cold calls. I need to put myself in front of people so I can sell my services and myself—just like I did with Jerry a year ago. I create flyers, brochures, and business cards, break out my receptionist outfits, and begin to troll the streets of Wilmington looking for clients. Door to door. Cold calls. In person.

My strategy is to enter every office building without a "No Soliciting" sign outside. I ask to talk to whomever manages the place. If that person isn't around, I leave a brochure and my business card, and make sure to call and follow up. If I'm lucky enough to connect with the right person, I ask if we can sit down for a few minutes. They usually agree. I outline Elite's services, our competitive prices, and what sets us apart from other cleaning companies. Though the operation is still just me and only me, I make sure to use the words "we" and "our" when describing the services. I want to come across as a legitimate firm that can deliver an excellent product. The people I'm meeting don't need to know their building will be cleaned by the company's CEO and sole employee—a harried twenty-one-year-old new mother trying desperately to begin a career.

I never stopped feeling disappointed in myself when I would solicit new customers and get rejected. But it also fueled me to keep trying. I kept hearing that "for every ten times you get a no, you'll get one yes," so I turned it into a numbers game. I figured that if I just made more calls, something good would happen. All I had to do was try, and the business would come to me.

I also had another reason for trying so hard. I was the only one in my family who didn't graduate from college. Going from high school right into marriage and babies looked like a recipe for an unsuccessful life. Inside, I had a deep fear of failure. The thought of how I would look to everyone else was humiliating to me. So I had no choice but to keep trying until something worked. I learned along the way that failing doesn't mean you won't succeed—it just means you tried something that didn't work. And so you try harder, or try something different, or just try again.

My motto was "Fail fast, then move on." Still is.

I continue to clean Bill and Jerry's building at night while taking care of Ryan and soliciting new clients all day. My husband and I are stressed over my lost income, so I need to make something good happen fast. It's discouraging to reach out to so many potential clients and get no response. But I am committed to my business, so I can't give up. That's not an option.

One day, after months of trying to land a single client, my persistence finally pays off. Someone I had solicited calls and offers me a contract. Great—except it's more work than I can possibly handle alone. He owns a medical complex of three separate buildings. I agree to the job before I even take the time to process what I'm in for. This new client has just tripled my workload. There's no way I can do it. It's time to hire someone to help me out.

As soon as I sign on the dotted line, my entire business strategy shifts. I now need to find employees who I can train to do as good a job as I do, so we can establish our reputation and live up to our name. If I have good people working for me, I figure, I can devote my time to pitching new clients. I am starting to feel more like a business owner than an hourly cleaning lady.

Walter, my first employee, is my polar opposite. He's an older gentleman who has a pretty serious demeanor. On first meeting, you might even describe him as grumpy. Despite that, he is an amazing worker. He always shows up and works hard. I love his dedication and loyalty. Without him by my side, I wouldn't be able to handle Bill and Jerry's building *and* the new client. Walter stays at Elite for the next eleven years. On his last day of work, he has a stroke. His wife calls from the hospital to let me know his condition, but Walter refuses to let me visit—his pride won't permit me to see him so ill. He never leaves the hospital.

To honor his contribution to Elite, I create an award in his name to go to my best employee each year. From Walter I learned an important lesson—I need to recognize the workers who go above and beyond.

By no means was cleaning offices and bathrooms my big dream in life. But my goal was to build a business that would support me and my family. That has never changed. I wanted to create a company that does something really well and makes a difference, however humble, in the world. With the help of great people who I love and admire, I'm still making that dream come true. I'm proud of what I do. It satisfies something inside me. Every day I set my goals a little higher, for a little more than I ever thought I would achieve, and that motivates me and gives me something new to shoot for. Every day.

You know the saying, "You don't know what you don't know"? Well, I had no idea how to do what I was doing, if that makes any sense. I didn't have the time or the money or the luxury of learning how to start a business before I started one. I was winging it constantly, every day. Somehow, though, little by little, I learned. I asked a lot of people who had experience in business, and from them I figured out basic things like how to come up with a bid—how to determine all the costs involved in a job, so I'd know what to charge for it. Eventually, I created formulas that calculated my costs of labor, taxes, insurance, supplies, health care, overhead, and allowed me to make a fair profit. That sounds like something you should know before you start. It took me years to figure it out.

Along the way, I lost money on jobs. But I made money, too.

CHERYL'S TIP FOR SUCCESS:
It's in the Timing

I fully believe that we as women can achieve anything we want, but we need to realize that it may not be all at the same time and done as perfectly as we want. Don't allow fear and self-doubt to stop you from stepping forward and achieving your goals when you know deep down that you can do it. It's all about the timing.

CHAPTER 3

Slow and Steady

"Just don't stop moving."

That's what I tell myself each morning during the early days of running Elite. Between managing the business and being a mom and wife, I am in constant motion.

For the first few years, the business has been growing steadily. I have several new clients and a handful of employees. If I can keep up the pace, I project to have about fifteen clients and twenty employees by year three. It's nice to have other people to help clean offices, but I'm still working way more than a normal human being, even after I've hung up my mop and bucket for the day. I still drop by our cleaning sites a few nights a week to make sure my employees are doing their job, and when it's necessary, I'll run a vacuum or dust some light fixtures. By day, I'm running around Wilmington soliciting potential clients, attending networking groups and Chamber of Commerce events, stopping by businesses to drop off marketing materials, and making a lot of cold calls on the phone.

With each new client I land, I have to hire more workers, which is becoming a full-time job in itself. Now I have to juggle scheduling, too, come up with fair employee policies and procedures, and keep the cash flow running smoothly so I can meet payroll and pay our expenses.

But what I really love about my business is the thrill of making the sale. Every new opportunity that comes my way excites me. When I get a yes, it feels great. I can look at the list of clients I've earned over the years, people who have stayed with me, and I know that I've served them well and made a difference in their lives. It's a high.

That doesn't mean my job is all pleasure. At times, it can be very stressful, and the thrill of making sales is just one part of what I have to do. There's a long list of other things to worry over—finances, employees, outside forces beyond my control. I can go from the high of a sale to the anxiety of some crisis in a matter of minutes.

I hit a tough spot when a valued client begins

bouncing checks. I know in business it should be all about the dollars and cents, particularly when I am paying people to clean for this client, but it's not that simple. I have a close, trusting relationship with him, and I feel a debt of gratitude. He took a chance on me when I was just getting started. He was one of the few people to respond to those marketing letters I sent, and he was trusting enough to give me not one but four buildings at two different sites. I couldn't believe my luck and accepted right away. His leap of faith in hiring Elite was one of the first signals to me that starting a commercial cleaning company wasn't completely insane.

For the first several months, everything ran smoothly. I was able to bank on that steady income, enabling me to hire more staff and get more ambitious in my marketing. Adding four buildings to our roster empowered me, and I reached out to even more accounts. We were rolling, or so I thought.

And then the bank notified me that their checks were being returned for insufficient funds. I wasn't concerned at first, understanding the intricacies of cash flow. It's not unusual for a company to run short from time to time. I overlooked the first few nonpayments. But this kept happening, month after month, until my own cash flow was compromised. I needed to figure out what to do.

I talked to the manager there who initially hired us. He listened as I detailed how many checks bounced. I expressed my worries about continuing the contract, but I also acknowledged that I was reluctant to drop such a big account.

"I'd love to keep working for you," I said, "as long as we get paid."

"Cheryl," the manager said, "if you hang in there, you'll see that the owners are out of cash and will have to file for bankruptcy. Once the bank takes over, you'll get paid. Just be patient."

I took in this advice. I thought about the consequences of not getting paid for several more months. It would knock a serious hole in us financially and risk putting my own company in danger of going under. But getting all that money they owed would be a big deal. And I wanted to keep the account even after the owners were forced to sell. It was a tough dilemma, but I had to make a choice.

And then I had an idea.

"What would you think of Elite moving its office into one of the vacant buildings in the complex we clean?" I asked. "I could credit our rent toward your outstanding invoices. I think it might be a win-win. My office space is way too cramped right now, and I'd love to have the physical space to grow."

The manager loved this idea and offered me the pick of any place in the complex. I found a space with four modestly sized offices, a break room, a bathroom, and a reception area. The move helped me feel like I was going places. The new space certainly felt business-like to me, and I was thrilled to work in such nice digs. I absolutely wanted the cash they owed me, but brokering this deal made me feel like at least I was recouping some of my loss.

Even as my role at Elite changes with every new client we gain, I am continually humbled by what it is my company actually does and by the hard work of my staff. A recent night cleaning reminds me that this can be a very grimy job.

I report to an office complex to clean with a female employee after the two other people on her crew call out. I show up dressed in my cleaning clothes and wheeling a cart containing our supplies, tired after a long day at work but ready to go. This is the life of a boss—every job is yours.

My colleague and I spend hours cleaning windows, vacuuming floors, and all the rest. Finally, at the end of the night, we take the fourteen bags of trash we've collected outside to the dumpster, finished at last with our shift. We struggle to open the dumpster door, which seems to be jammed. So we decide to hoist the trash bags over our heads and into the dumpster opening on top.

Not an easy task. But we get them in there, one by one. We have just a few bags left when my colleague tosses one and, instead of going inside the dumpster, it explodes in midair. The bag's entire contents pour all over us. Naturally, it was a bag of kitchen trash. Food scraps rain down on us as we stand there in shock. But then we begin to laugh because what else can we do? I look over at her—she's laughing hysterically, and I can see that she has coffee grounds in her teeth. Now we have to clean up this mess. Covered in half-eaten food, we pick up all the trash and get it into the dumpster.

It's nights like these that remind me that showing appreciation to my staff as well as my clients is key to running a successful business.

&

I am finding similarities between motherhood and my role at Elite. Both can be extremely gratifying at times and overwhelming otherwise. My husband and I are slowly getting into our groove following Ryan's birth, though we have to work hard at finding balance between our jobs and our home life. He is self-employed as an appraiser, so we're both operating small businesses. We're constantly juggling work, childcare, and family time, especially since a few nights a week I'm out visiting our work sites. At the beginning of our marriage, I was the one waiting at home for him to finish work. Now it's my husband waiting for me, feeding Ryan, giving him his bath, and putting him to bed. We don't talk much about the stress in our lives, but it's there all the time.

In spite of the focus on our careers, we are eager to spend weekends on family time. Fridays are usually at home with homemade pizza and a movie, and Ryan gets to have a sleepover in our bedroom, placing his sleeping bag on the floor. On Saturdays, we hang out with friends at some event or at a restaurant. We go to church most Sunday mornings and spend time at my parents' pool in summer. My brother often brings his family, too, and it's fun to watch Ryan swim and play with his cousins. My younger sister left the area to attend college in the Midwest, and I miss her a lot. But my schedule doesn't really allow me to spend as much time with other people as I'd like.

As Elite grows, so does our income. I decide to splurge and purchase a BMW—partly because I want to present myself to clients as a success but also as a reward for all my hard work. Before long, we think we might be ready to move to a bigger house in a better school district. My husband and I also discuss adding to our family. I haven't been in a rush to have another child. I feel like I have plenty of time for that—I was young when I had Ryan, and I don't hear my biological clock ticking yet. But there's another reason—my husband and I are so wrapped up in our jobs and Ryan's life that it's hard to imagine adding anything extra.

We begin to search for our perfect new home. Ryan is nearing kindergarten, and my husband and I are both eager for more space and a nicer environment. We want to live somewhere that reflects all our hard work and is maybe a little aspirational—a reach. Living in a home that inspires us to keep striving and earning will certainly keep us focused on our businesses.

After some time driving through neighborhoods, checking out listings, and going to open houses, we decide to build a semi-custom home in Hockessin, Delaware. The neighborhood has a real community feeling, and the neighbors are also raising young children. I am in awe that my husband and I are able to make this happen. Weren't we just starting out as young newlyweds? Has it really been almost six years since Ryan was born? It's starting to feel like we're now making some of our dreams about family and financial security come true.

&

Elite grows significantly in the first few years. I am grateful that it runs smoothly more often than not. There are times when I make mistakes, and when forces out of my control affect the business. For a time, I have a partner, but it becomes clear fairly soon that my hunger for running the company is greater than hers. I buy her out and begin to picture what's next. I have a growing company, a committed workforce, and the drive to succeed.

What I *don't* have is a sophisticated business plan or a college degree, so I rely on my intuition and work ethic. I would love to connect with other CEOs to get ideas and advice, but this is easier said than done. One of my biggest breakthroughs in creating a client-focused culture occurs randomly one day. I am strolling through the MBNA buildings that we clean in downtown Wilmington. The bank controls several buildings with tower bridges connecting them.

I am struck by the motivational messages the company displays throughout its cluster of buildings, especially one that reads, "If better is possible, then good is not good enough." I stare at the sign and realize I need to make this the heart of Elite. I want my clients to know how dedicated my employees are to their needs. It's how I've felt about the company since the first day cleaning Bill and Jerry's building. I want to strive for excellence and prove my worth to clients. This attitude must unite my employees, whether they are cleaning in the evenings or answering phones during the day. I decide then and there to adopt this motto and make it Elite's signature philosophy. To this day, I stress to my employees that we have to be the best that clients can get for their money. It's what keeps them happy and referring us to others.

Elite's commitment to excellence is just one thing that sets the company apart from our competitors. The fact that I run the company makes it unique in the industry as well. In the early 1990s, I am one of very few women running a commercial cleaning services firm. I generally compete for clients against men, and sometimes lose out to them because I am not part of the boys' club. This reality sometimes gets to me and makes me angry and frustrated. I try my best to let it roll off my back and keep moving forward because that's the only goal that counts. It would be easier, I realize, to move into residential cleaning, where so many women run businesses and succeed. I even dabble in this area with Elite, but my heart is in commercial cleaning—a bigger and more lucrative (and more competitive) arena. Negotiating with and serving these large businesses run by hard-nosed managers is what lights my fire.

By year six with Elite, I am feeling pretty good about how far I've come. I'm no longer the shy secretary at the mercy of her bosses' wishes and whims. Now I, too, am a small business owner driving my own future. At that moment, I realize that Elite is giving me the life I've always wanted. But life never stays so simple for very long.

Five years after giving birth to Ryan, my husband and I decide to add to our family. Elite is providing reliable income, and I have been able to hire, train, and build trust with my team. We are thrilled when I become pregnant, especially because Ryan is now in grade school and more independent every day. It's satisfying how different my life is during this pregnancy. I'm no longer living paycheck to paycheck, working as a daytime receptionist and nighttime cleaning lady.

Despite that, not everything is easy. I'm not sick enough to slack off at work, but I never feel 100 percent well. Granted, I'm six years older this time, but my energy lags, and by the final months of my pregnancy I decide it's time to slow down on selling our services. The company is in a good position to sustain itself for a while, and I need to make it through this pregnancy before I can begin to focus on what's next.

The final month is much more complicated than it was with Ryan. Prior to the delivery, the doctors tell me that the baby is in the frank breech position. This means instead of head down, its legs are pointed upward, folded over its body. This will require me to have a C-section. I had absolutely no complications when delivering Ryan, and this news makes me nervous. I begin to worry about my own recovery, not to mention the health of my baby.

On November 17, 1994, Erica arrives via C-section. The delivery is smooth, but I accept the reality that I'll be healing for much longer than when I had my first child. No other complications, though. A few days later, my husband and I drive Erica home, ready to begin life as a family of four.

CHERYL'S TIP FOR SUCCESS:
Focus on Your Values

Even without a business education, I knew early on that Elite needed to live up to certain values to gain and retain clients. I loved using slogans like "If better is possible, then good is not good enough" to instill the right values and mindset among my employees. We have always gone the extra mile for clients, whether it means picking up phones on the first ring, doing extra cleaning services without being asked, or accommodating new requests. Even today, I uphold these values for Elite and use every opportunity to share them with clients, too: We stand for quality, collaboration, sustainability, responsiveness, integrity, and safety. These core values have helped me grow the company, which is now in eighteen states and employs more than 750 workers.

CHAPTER 4

Challenges

The first month with Erica home is a blur, including the usual sleepless nights and endless diaper changes. I am also caring for my own body after the C-section, meaning I can't climb stairs or drive as soon as I had hoped. And I need to give six-year-old Ryan enough attention so he doesn't think the new baby will cut in on his time with me.

At the same time, I'm still a businesswoman. There's something I built that I can't allow to languish even now. Elite is constantly in the back of my mind. I yearn to get back to that, too, and find a new normal that allows me to be a mother, a wife, and an entrepreneur.

But life has other plans for me. During our visit to the pediatrician when Erica is a month old, the doctor says something is concerning. Her eyes are swaying outward, he says. Generally, it's not unusual for a newborn to cross her eyes, he tells us, but this movement could also be a sign that something needs correction. For parents of a new baby, even the smallest things can cause worry, like too much spit-up, not enough diaper changes, fussy behavior. Learning that your child may have a real medical issue is a jolt to the heart. I feel the tears well up and my throat go dry with the news that something might be wrong.

The pediatrician refers us for an MRI and to a pediatric ophthalmologist to get some answers. Nothing unusual appears on the scan. As the eye doctor examines my little baby, I feel rattled. Like every new mother, I imagined Erica's life as a newborn would only be filled with the usual happy moments. I wanted to rock her to sleep, kiss her head, and dress her up in frilly pink outfits. Going in and out of doctors' offices during her first few months of life is not what I had in mind.

After an examination, the doctor has a diagnosis: Erica has an eye muscle issue. It's not serious, but it needs treatment. If she doesn't get it corrected, her brain will stop sending communication to the eye, a scary thought. She'll need to wear an eye patch for several hours a day until the muscle strengthens.

I am relieved that it isn't anything more serious. I feel like once we fix her eye, the condition will be a distant memory. And after a few months at home with the baby, I'm ready to get back to work full-time. My husband and I figured out childcare, and we're finding our way, juggling work and kids. I had to step back at work a few months before Erica's birth and now I'm eager to see my employees in the office and at our sites on a daily basis. I'm also feeling the pressure to keep the money coming into our household budget.

But there's a problem with my plan. Throughout her first year of her life, Erica struggles with her health, and of course so do we. Our baby is constantly developing pneumonia. Watching this little girl struggle to breathe is agonizing. I feel like as soon as she starts to seem better, she takes a turn for the worse and ends up with pneumonia again. During every pediatrician visit, I press the doctor about what is causing this. But we get no answers.

By the fourth or fifth bout with pneumonia, the doctor begins to offer some guesses about why Erica keeps getting sick.

"Maybe it's because she was born via C-section that she has extra mucus in her lungs," he says. Or,

"It's probably just because she's a winter baby. They get sick more and need to build up their immune systems."

But it isn't just the pneumonia and the eye condition making me nervous about Erica. There are other signs that something isn't right. I can see that she isn't keeping up with baby milestones. This is apparent when flipping through parenting magazines or watching my friends' kids. Erica can't sit or balance herself. She's small for her age. The pediatrician refers us to a geneticist because Erica isn't even registering on the growth charts for height and weight. The geneticist takes our family history and decides that Erica resembles her father's side of the family, where some of the women are not even five feet tall.

I am still not satisfied that everything is fine with my daughter. I need better answers.

One day in the pediatrician's office, I decide it's time to be pushy. Erica is now eighteen months old and still not walking. Her crawling is helping her reach places and become more mobile, but she drags her legs. I am not getting the impression that she'll be walking anytime soon.

"I need you to take a closer look at Erica and

give me some answers about why she is not walking," I say. "I know she is not on track. I see it with my own eyes."

The doctor dismisses my request. "There is nothing to worry about right now, Cheryl. She has other issues we need to focus on. Calm down and relax about her walking. She'll do it eventually. All kids are on their own timetable."

This "answer" is all I hear from the pediatrician about Erica's development. But I also get a referral to a pulmonologist to see about why her pneumonia won't go away.

Confronting the pediatrician a year and a half after Erica was born is the first time it hits me that I have to be her strongest advocate. To the doctors, she's just another patient and I'm just another anxious mother. But she is my child and a driving force in my life. My gut tells me that I need to push harder.

☙

I'm waiting nervously beside Erica in a hospital room. In a few minutes she'll get a barium swallow test, the second major exam she has undergone since we met with the pulmonologist. During our first visit, the doctor expressed concern about Erica's development, much more than our pediatrician ever did. She asked me right away why Erica wasn't walking. It was a jolt to hear the urgency in her voice. It validated my own anxious feelings but also raised some even scarier possibilities.

First, the pulmonologist suspected that Erica might have cystic fibrosis and ordered her to undergo a test for it. By now I was terrified. Cystic fibrosis is a life-threatening diagnosis, I thought, one that I was not prepared for. Thankfully, she tested negative for it and we could put that diagnosis aside (even though they had to do the test twice).

Next, Erica is prepped for the barium test. I wait to be called in to observe once it begins. This time they'll look at her gastrointestinal system, to see if reflux is causing the endless cycle of pneumonia. My hands sweat and I nervously tap my toes as I wait to be called in. I hear the clock tick and nothing else. I try to stay focused on the here and now, but my mind races ahead.

I'm summoned in to watch the radiologist perform the test and support Erica. Halfway through the procedure, the radiologist gets up and abruptly leaves the room, seeming perplexed. I look over at the nurse and ask her what is going on. She has no idea, she says. We wait silently for the doctor to return. The worries I had before the test now multiply by ten. *What is going on?*

The radiologist eventually returns and reassures me that Erica did well and he got what he needed. But he doesn't explain any details, and neither does he say why he ran out of the room. We'll know the test results soon, he tells me, so Erica and I go home to wait. In the back of my mind, I'm certain there's something he's not telling me, and it has to do with his quick exit during the examination.

Finally, I get the call. Something *did* show up during Erica's exam, but not at all what we were expecting. She's so small that the abdomen X-ray also showed her hips, and the radiologist immediately noticed that something was seriously wrong: Erica's hips were dislocated.

Soon after this revelation, the pediatrician calls me to confirm the news and schedule a follow-up exam. I'm in shock—all I can think of is how many times he blew me off when I raised the issue of Erica not walking. All I want now is to know what we need to do to make our daughter healthy again.

Erica's condition, known as bilateral hip dysplasia, is extremely prevalent in babies born in the frank breech position, we learn. This is because the baby's bottom is near the birth canal and its head is at the top of the placenta, with legs bent over the body and face. Most often, these babies will be evaluated immediately following birth for ailments including scoliosis, clubbed feet, and bilateral hip dysplasia. No one examined Erica for any of these conditions. And to make the situation even more frustrating, *had* the doctor diagnosed her condition then, it could have been corrected with a brace that she would have worn for just six weeks. And it would have been fixed!

Instead, Erica isn't diagnosed until well into her second year of life. She is much bigger now, and her body has adjusted to the dislocated hips. Her groin tendons are too tight, and fixing the problem will require significant medical intervention.

Correcting Erica's condition becomes a nightmarish process. The doctors first suggest using a cast to hold Erica's legs in a frog-like position. I feel like this is just an attempt to cover for our pediatrician, who completely missed our daughter's diagnosis. Nevertheless, we agree to try. Six months later, the doctors remove the cast to see if it helped. It didn't.

At almost two years old, Erica now must undergo major surgery. This requires rebuilding the sockets around her femur, adding plates and screws, and grafting bone. Not only that, but then, for six months, she has to live inside a whole-body cast, which has to then be redone several times so the doctors can reset her legs. I am in constant amazement at my brave little daughter during this ordeal. She is so tough, rarely crying or screaming out, except when the electric saw blade comes near to cut off her cast. The noise frightens me, too. Once the cast comes off, she has yet another procedure. This cycle goes on and on, but Erica always shows maturity beyond her years.

When Erica was in the hospital, I spent every night with her. I felt guilty about not being home with my son, but I couldn't leave her there alone. She would become very quiet in the hospital and rarely talked. It was no fun for a scared little girl. They would put her on the same floor as the children with cancer—a grim environment, which put things into perspective. Our issues were life-altering but not life-threatening. Not that this made things any easier for Erica or for me.

I spent many nights in the hospital by Erica's

bedside. Despite the agony of the situation, I was always grateful that we could take her home. Many parents of children in pediatric hospitals never go home with their child. I also felt so appreciative that a renowned children's hospital was in our community and that Erica, her father, and I could make the frequent trips necessary without arduous, expensive travel.

The process of correcting Erica's bilateral hip dysplasia is not only physically painful but also an emotional strain. It interferes with other aspects of her development. Most toddlers her age are running around at the park, rummaging through their toy boxes, and learning to talk, go potty, and feed themselves. The intensity of Erica's medical procedures prevents all that, requiring even more medical intervention—speech therapy, plus lots of physical therapy. She bonds with her physical therapist Noelle, who she calls "Ohwell." They develop quite a friendship, and Erica bargains with Ohwell when the procedures are exhausting and seemingly impossible. But Erica loves aqua therapy, and that becomes a major bargaining chip as she recovers from surgery and the many follow-up procedures required to repair her body.

ॐ

Following Erica's diagnosis and subsequent surgeries, my husband and I spend the next five or so years managing all our responsibilities and caring for our daughter. Of course, we also have to raise our son, who at eight is just starting to have a life of his own. We want him to play sports and spend time with friends, so my husband takes him while I care for Erica. I am still running Elite, but I have very little time or energy for growing the business. A child with special needs requires constant care, and I am never able to pause Erica's many medical and emotional needs while I take care of work. Being my own boss has advantages, as I am able to run Elite and manage Erica's constant surgeries, hospital stays, rehabilitation, and more.

Ryan was almost six when Erica was born, and he was already an active, athletic little guy. We took him to an ice rink when he was three and he loved it so much that by four, he was playing hockey. Between that, school, and playing with the neighborhood kids, he was busy living his life. So when Erica was going through her medical issues, I never sensed that he was jealous of all the attention she received. But I felt guilty because I wasn't as involved in my son's life as I should have been, or wanted to be. It was hard to get Erica out of the house—often, she was in a body cast or wheelchair, or using a walker. So she and I stayed home, meaning I missed a lot of Ryan's life, watching him play soccer and hockey.

He didn't like coming to the hospital to visit Erica —understandably, it was very upsetting to see his sister in that condition. Once, when he did come, he spent a little time with Erica but then quickly found another boy his age on her floor, a cancer patient, and played with him. When we left, I could tell something was bothering Ryan. He asked me why the little boy had lost his hair and whether he would live.

Adjusting to life after Erica's surgeries was more complicated than just taking her home. It was only after her first operation, when she was put into a full-body cast, that we realized we couldn't leave the hospital until we got a customized car seat. It quickly became apparent that Erica's medical issues would not be resolved easily.

Part of the ordeal was financial. When the hospital administrators first brought up Medicaid, I got pretty sensitive. My husband and I were proud to be self-made and assumed our family health insurance plans would cover Erica's expenses. The hospital staff knew better. They explained that a child with our daughter's medical needs could send us into financial ruin without outside help.

After her surgery and six months in a full cast, Erica had to rely on a state-sponsored program for school. She couldn't go to just any daycare because of the assistance she needed to get around. Erica used a wheelchair and then hip braces during her recovery, and the program offered her transportation to and from school. It allowed her to be with other kids and learn social skills. Erica had had a rough start in life, and I was determined that she have a full childhood, so a program like this was important to her development. At school, Erica was able to interact both with kids who also have special needs and kids without them. The school gave her a wonderful, sympathetic environment.

We also must adapt at home to meet her needs. My in-laws stay with us to provide support for Erica but also for my husband, our son, and me. Our daughter requires constant attention. I can't just leave her in her crib while I take a shower, the way I did with Ryan at that age. We can't sit in the living room while she plays in the kitchen with her toys.

It takes years of surgery and follow-up appointments for Erica's life to get any easier. We try to inch back to a traditional family life, but often I feel like the cards are stacked against us.

For instance, one summer a few years after Erica's initial surgery, we decide to visit to the beach for a family vacation. We couldn't travel at all while Erica was receiving her most intensive medical care, in her early years. So this was going to be a long-overdue treat. My husband and I took a leap and booked a vacation home in Ocean City, Maryland. It wasn't an over-the-top plan, as the beach is just a few hours away, but it felt so normal and even luxurious after what we'd been through.

A few days before we are set to leave, Erica begins to complain that her leg hurts. We think that the pain is from running outside that day, and we put her to bed and hope she feels better in the morning. The next day Erica is screaming, and we race to the hospital to find out what's wrong. The doctors can't find anything unusual, so they send us home, even though Erica is still in pain. We begin to pack for our vacation, but a day before the trip begins, we notice Erica is now limping. We take her back to the hospital and learn that, once again, the doctors missed something. This time an X-ray shows a hairline fracture in her leg. They put Erica in a body cast to repair it, leaving her with one leg free. We desperately want to keep our plans for a vacation, so we head to the beach, feeling optimistic that we can make this work.

Unfortunately, Erica's free leg still has an incision from a prior surgery, which gets infected a few days into our trip. She and I leave the beach to head back to the hospital.

As Erica gets older, she requires fewer doctor's appointments, but life is never carefree for her. Her body sometimes struggles to recover from medical procedures and even common childhood illnesses. She's just a girl who needs more care. I think of how far she's come and how tough she is, and that helps me reconcile all that's happened to her. Though I never expected life to be perfect or that being a parent would always be easy, the challenges have given me immense appreciation for Erica and for all those who helped us get through a very difficult time.

Being a parent of a child with special needs is exhausting, unrelenting, and often lonely. During Erica's early years, I would feel uncomfortable taking her out because of how people would react.

I vividly remember taking her to one of Ryan's baseball games, and she and I were like a sideshow. People watched us, yet no one came over to talk. Yes, it was unusual to see a young child in a body cast, but we were still just another family at a baseball game, supporting our Little Leaguer. Any of those parents could have chatted about the boys or even asked how Erica was doing. But they never did. I remember counting the outs of the game, waiting impatiently for it to end so we could make a beeline for the car. When I think back, I realize that I didn't stay home with Erica only because leaving the house was logistically so complicated. I just didn't like how I felt at Ryan's baseball game.

If you see a family with a special needs child, talk to them. Don't let them feel that they should be ignored. They are just like you, trying to make it in a tough, sometimes insensitive world. Connect with the parents and try to communicate with the child. It is likely that they'll be grateful. I remember feeling so emotionally drained during those early years with Erica, and I would have been so happy to have a friendly conversation. I always try to approach families with special circumstances and give them the time and attention they deserve.

CHERYL'S TIP FOR SUCCESS:
Sometimes Real Life Comes First

That lattice—which allows you to move sideways and even a little backward when necessary—is what makes it possible for you to prioritize your role as a mother, a daughter, a wife, or a friend. Never feel as though these moments are setbacks. They're part of what make you who you are, as a human being but also as a person with dreams of success.

Strain

As we approach Erica's fifth birthday, following all her surgeries and recoveries, my family and I are able to settle into a somewhat normal routine. My in-laws have moved out of our house. We now string together weeks and months without any emergencies that split our time between home, work, and hospital. We four enjoy all the normal celebrations and fun now that things have calmed down. We love to mark the end of each week by going out for dinner. We even take a vacation in Cancun, where we swim, walk the beaches, relax, and spend time together.

Ryan is nearing the end of elementary school. He has quite a bit going on. We're either running him to a sports practice or game or helping him with his homework. Erica is preparing for kindergarten. She attends a special preschool that meets her needs and helps prepare her for the transition to what's next. It is such a relief to see her with her peers, learning and socializing. After so many years spent in and out of hospitals, with no light at the end of the tunnel, seeing her thrive in school brings me such joy. We still spend a fair amount of time visiting doctors, of course, but we're no longer living according to the surgeon's schedule.

With the kids in school, I'm finally able to focus on Elite. Maintaining the business during Erica's most intense years was difficult. I was fortunate that my staff could step in when I was unavailable. Never once did I leave Erica's side when she needed me, so there were plenty of times I couldn't be in the office. Running a business without an active CEO strained the company at times, but we maintained a steady stream of new clients. My focus during these years was just to manage the basic needs of the company: meeting payroll, paying the bills, sending out bids, and keeping the paperwork moving forward. I wasn't able to think about Elite's future or the growth of the company. I was just thankful to have a business.

℘

The settled rhythm of life doesn't last long, though. While I am thrilled to be back in the office and pouring myself into Elite, my husband doesn't feel the same way about his career. One day, not long before Erica's fifth birthday, he proposes a radical change—that we move to Florida.

I am stunned but not completely surprised. We are well into the second decade of our marriage, and it's been an eventful ride so far. It's easy to lose your path as a couple when you're raising kids, and having two of them five years apart—and one with serious medical needs—has given us little time together. We're no longer two teenagers in love. We rarely communicate beyond working out the week's schedule. Talking about our hopes and dreams is a distant memory.

My husband used to say that he wasn't doing what he really wanted to do with his life. He wasn't only dissatisfied with me—it was everything. He said he had wanted to be an architect, but his parents gave him a choice of two colleges, neither of which offered the necessary courses.

I finally asked him, "Why didn't you just go where you wanted and pay for college yourself? Or take night courses and get your degree?"

He had no answer. I felt like I was to blame for his unhappiness.

The urge to move to Florida might be a good way to shift gears, I thought. But I was unsure that the tension in our marriage would go away simply by heading south. However, the timing felt right, with Erica about to start elementary school and Ryan moving into middle school very soon. I decided to remain open to his proposal and was hopeful that relocating might be the change my husband needed.

The Florida idea gains momentum in the next few months. My husband is totally dedicated to the idea of us starting fresh. I am less enthusiastic, but I'm not opposed to living in nice weather year-round. The discussions surrounding our move never quite encompass the big picture, but over time we make several small decisions to get the transition going. We put our house on the market. We decide that we'll open an ice cream store down there. We discuss the need for me to sell Elite.

This last detail is much more complicated than any of our other plans. Opening a business is much easier than leaving one. I know Elite is in a healthy place and could be sold for a fair amount of money. But getting to a final handoff will take some time.

Eager to execute his plan, my husband moves to Florida as soon as we sell our house. I need to stay put until I figure out what to do with Elite, so the kids and I move into my parents' home. I keep our daily routines going—school for them, work for me. Even with the support of my parents, I feel like a single mom. I'm making lunches, taking the kids to school, leaving work early for the bus drop-off, shuttling Ryan to activities, making dinner, and putting them to bed every night. I miss having a spouse and partner.

Selling a business isn't as simple as putting a yard sign in front of the office. I hire a consultant to help me figure out how to value Elite, and we meet several interested parties over the next few months. Often, I am frustrated by the process. Potential buyers keep submitting low-ball bids. The roller coaster of selling it makes me realize how personally attached I am to my company. I started Elite all by myself and have grown it into a successful firm with a large staff and presence in the community. It's hard to imagine giving it up—it's such a huge piece of me and has always provided for my family. I can't help but feel resentful about having to give up on it.

I'm not the only one having difficulties with our plan. My husband grows impatient with me as the kids and I remain in Delaware. He's been working on the business in Florida by himself and biding his time until we move down. He and I touch base on the phone, but it often feels like we are living very different lives. I am still tied to Elite and the kids. He is totally on his own, running a new business and trying to figure out where his family will fit in Florida. He begins to socialize and make some new friends. I don't know who he's meeting or what he's doing. Even though we've been married for so long and dedicated to our family, I am starting to feel all the negative effects of a long-distance relationship.

It becomes obvious *how* different our lives have become when I visit him in Florida after a few months apart. I realize that he's now essentially living a bachelor lifestyle, with new friends to go with it. I also suspect that one woman in particular may be more than a friend. The thought that he would be unfaithful hits me like a lightning bolt. While I've been keeping our kids in their routine and on track and trying to run and sell Elite simultaneously, he's moved to South Florida to start anew, under the pretense that it will be a good move for us all. I wonder if he even wants us to relocate or if he's too happy being free of marriage and fatherhood.

That wasn't the only problem. He thought a store selling ice cream and Italian ice would be a big success down there. But it wasn't happening. While there, I sometimes ran the shop, to give him a break, and the customers would tell me, "You guys are never open when the sign says you are." I think he didn't even show up some days.

I often felt that the responsibility for supporting the family was mine. Our situation was that we didn't share the same drive, passion, or determination. I don't mind working hard. In fact, I love it. I get excited when I reach a new goal or see the success that comes from working.

Visiting Florida opens my eyes to the mistake it would be for me to move here. Selling Elite and uprooting the family is not in my best interest nor in the best interest of my kids. I have made a life for myself in Wilmington, and leaving home and career for a new situation, where my husband is already living a single man's life, would be a disaster. Forcing the kids to leave school and lifelong friends would be painful for them. Finding new doctors for Erica that truly understand her medical needs would be detrimental to her health.

I depart Florida with open eyes. Once I get home, I start a plan to share this revelation with my husband.

∞

My hands sweat as I dial his number.

It's been a few weeks since I visited my husband down in Florida and realized that he's made a new life—for himself. Maybe he needed a change, but there is a lot going on for me in Delaware. Trying to sell Elite has shown me how much I care about it. I don't want to let it go. I call my husband to tell him my decision and give him the chance to reflect on our marriage and family. He needs to decide what he's going to do.

After a few rings, he answers the phone. I dive right into the speech I've rehearsed. I am not going to sell Elite. The kids and I are not going to move to Florida. He and I have to decide what we want to do based on that. I get my speech out and quickly end the call. I don't want him to respond right away. I want him to think about next steps before we talk again.

A few days go by. My stomach is in knots as I wait to hear from him. I'm going through my normal routine but in a fog. Finally he calls, and honestly, I am not sure what he's going to say. After some small talk discussing the kids, he gives me his decision: He's going to sell the business in Florida and move back home with us.

I am relieved that he's willing to make our marriage and family his top priority. But his decision is painful, too. The ice cream business drained our savings and he confesses to me that he had an affair. This could be a deal-breaker, but I'm willing to live with it for the sake of our family. I've missed having another parent in the mix for the last few months, and so I want to believe that we can work on our relationship—with some changes.

When my husband moves back north, however, life looks a lot different than when he left. We're all living with my parents now and have no resources to purchase a new home. Our savings are gone, and my husband has no job. I decide that the best thing would be for him to join me at Elite. He can be my right hand, helping with bookkeeping, data entry, bills, and payroll. That new role for him would help me out immensely. I need to hustle and get Elite some new clients, especially now that our family is entirely dependent on my earnings. Over the next few months we work and save, find a house, settle our kids into their schools, and begin again.

The new arrangement works smoothly. Knowing that my husband and I are recommitting to our marriage and our family lights a fire in me. I am ready to figure out what Elite needs to grow.

One key decision I make is to expand my staff. I can't be the jack of all trades and the visionary at the same time. The company is positioned to grow if I can find the way to make it happen. In addition to hiring my husband, I take on an operations manager and a salesperson.

But his role at Elite doesn't satisfy my husband for long. After celebrating our twentieth wedding anniversary, it becomes clear to me that he is growing restless again. He expresses his dissatisfaction in active and passive ways. Sometimes he talks about wanting to return to Florida to live. Or he'll say that he never imagined himself working for a cleaning business. (You can imagine how that went over with me.) Decisions are made at Elite without my knowledge and he changes decisions I have made without discussing it with me. He doesn't like that I am in charge and that he works for me. The tension between us grows at work and boils over at home.

One night, after a particularly bad scene between us, I decide to pack a bag and leave for the night. The kids are both at sleepovers, and I can't stand the thought of spending the night alone. I walk out in the middle of the fight, and by the time I put the key in the ignition, I feel completely done with my marriage.

As I drive away, I'm still not sure where I'm going or what I'm doing. I decide to call my dad. He's a minister and a rock to me and my mom, sister, and brother, so I know he'll give me good advice if I ask him to weigh in on this situation. I've never been too open with him about the troubles in my marriage, and I assume he'll encourage me to seek counseling or find a new way to try and make it work.

I pull up to my parents' house and my dad meets me by the pool. It's a warm night, and we sit outside as I unload all my feelings. I am not happy, I say. My husband is not happy. I don't want to be married any longer. My dad sits calmly and listens as I reel off story after story of what my life has been like for the last few years.

After I finish, my dad begins to speak. Instead of a pep talk about the sanctity of marriage, I get a surprising reply.

"Cheryl, honey," he says, "do you assume that your mom and I don't see these things, too? What's taken you so long to realize this? Your mother and I would rather see you alone and happy than married and miserable."

I am not looking for my dad's blessing for a divorce, but hearing him say those words gives me some new perspective. I *am* miserable. Others see it, too. I realize my kids must also see it. I know that I am not a miserable person, but I need to make some big changes to get back on track.

That night, I decide: It's time for me to take my life into my own hands and set a better path for myself and my kids. I am ready to begin a new chapter. I need to leave my marriage.

CHERYL'S TIP FOR SUCCESS:
You Can Always Change Your Mind

It's important to remember that in life, most decisions can be changed. I agreed to go along with my husband's idea to relocate to Florida because I truly thought it would help our family. But as time went on, I realized that was not the best plan for me or my kids. I was fortunate that my attempts to sell Elite took time, because it allowed me to evaluate this monumental decision with more scrutiny.

Though nixing the Florida plan and getting my husband back home did not save our marriage, we were able to put our life back together after selling our house and losing our savings with the failed ice cream business. Realize that at times, your first decision may not always be your best. Take a deep breath, sit back, and reevaluate your situation. It's okay to change your mind, your course, or your path. And remember that tough times don't have to stay that way.

&

CHAPTER 6

The Meltdown

The talk with my dad crystalizes the feelings I've had about my marriage. But divorce, especially when kids are involved, takes time. There's a lot to untangle after twenty-three years.

I resolve to begin the process, even if it's not obvious at first. My husband remains at home, and we are able to peacefully coexist for the sake of the kids. Ryan is entering his senior year of high school, and my husband and I would like to keep things as normal as possible for him while he graduates and chooses a college. I know we'll have to find a way to manage the breakup for Erica's sake. I'm not eager to jump into the single life. Taking baby steps seems like the right way to go.

Despite our best efforts, though, living under one roof proves challenging for my husband and me. It's not always possible to stuff down your negative feelings. At Ryan's commencement ceremony, my husband and I are barely speaking, except to fight. The strain makes it difficult to enjoy our son's big day. I am constantly battling the negativity that surrounds our shattered marriage, trying to pull myself away from pessimism and frustration. Navigating these intense emotional waters takes away from the joy I feel for Ryan, though I put up a happy front for our loved ones. I don't want my drama to loom over our kids' lives.

My husband was still working for me at Elite, so we saw each other for hours each day. Even work didn't provide an escape. I tried to keep my distance in the office and was thankful I could travel to work sites, sales meetings, and other outside events. Keeping Elite stable and profitable was important even as my personal life was falling apart. Our family's livelihood was 100 percent dependent on my keeping the business strong. I refused to let my anguish get in the way of Elite's success. I showed up every day ready to go, trying to stay as optimistic as possible. But I'm only human.

A physical separation does finally come, almost a year after I had decided to end the marriage. My husband, realizing he can't keep working for me, decides to take computer courses to train for a new career. He moves out of our house to live with a friend from school. Soon, he finds a new job, and at last we are no longer forced together day after day. Life is moving on.

We start mediation in hopes of resolving the divorce as painlessly as possible. There's a lot to sort out. Because I am the breadwinner, my husband wants me to pay him alimony. We also have to divide up our marital assets, and I'll have to buy his share of our home if I want to keep living there. We have to manage child support and custody, too. And I need to protect Elite and make sure it doesn't get split up during the proceedings as I am the sole owner of the company. There's quite a bit at stake.

I celebrate my fortieth birthday with friends and family in New York City at around the same time my husband moves out. Even though I am sad about the end of married life, I feel hopeful that I'll be in a better place soon. I am surrounded by loving people on this trip to the Big Apple, and the weekend of fun reminds me that I deserve a joyful, fulfilling life.

And then, of course, just as I'm feeling good about the future, things start getting ugly. Maybe trying to remain civil during our first year apart made the present worse. Maybe it would be difficult no matter what I did. But within six months, we are both spending thousands of dollars on legal fees. The lawyers are now exchanging constant accusations, demands, untruths. I feel under attack, defending my character, my children, and my business. It's like I'm struggling to swim upstream while the current is dragging me down.

My sister Vicki and my friend Jill are on speed dial during this difficult time. I call them almost daily to recount the twists and turns of the proceedings. I cry, yell, and scream while I try to process the behavior of the person who was my husband for more than twenty years. It's unbelievable that we once loved each other and wanted a life together. Those hours spent on Little League sidelines, at family dinners, on vacations are distant, unreal memories. I am grateful that Vicki and Jill are always willing to listen to me. There's no way I could keep these feelings bottled up inside.

I'm lucky enough to meet other women also going through divorce. When we talk, I realize that we're all in similar situations, but my drama is ten times worse than most. And believe me, this is not something I am proud of!

Months into the divorce proceedings, I get wind that my husband has one of his family members footing his legal bills. This relative has nearly unlimited funds, so the back-and-forth between our lawyers could last forever. While I am sweating over the invoices from my attorney, I realize that this has become a game, and we're throwing a very costly ball back and forth over the net. I am starting to worry that there will be nothing left for me financially when this nightmare finally comes to an end.

Erica's needs force my ex and me to interact regularly. I'm open to the possibility of sharing custody, as I want her to have a relationship with her father. We work out an arrangement where she spends one night every week and every other weekend with him. But this never turns into a routine. My ex regularly changes his plans or his mind about when to take her. It ultimately requires a judge threatening him about losing custody altogether to get him to stick to the schedule.

Thankfully, Ryan is away at college and doesn't have to witness all this. Erica and I have a strong bond from our years spent in and out of hospitals. I try to make up for the conflict by giving her as much stability as I can. I'm fiercely protective of her and want her to have a normal, happy life. We still have to manage her health regularly, but we also spend evenings playing games and coloring. We laugh a lot. Erica is a funny child, and her sense of humor can bring out the laughter in me.

I must also keep Elite functioning normally during the divorce. It needs my focus in spite of the time and energy I have to spend elsewhere. I resolve to stay as professional as possible, but there are times when it's just impossible for me to persevere as I would like. Thank goodness for my team and my amazing operations manager. I am proud of how hard they work to keep the business afloat while I am unavailable. Elite's focus on core values and principles keeps my employees motivated to maintain our standards. Though the company doesn't grow much during this time, it maintains its good reputation and stays on course—unlike me, who often can't think straight.

The stress of divorce takes a toll on my mind and my body. I lose a lot of weight and have trouble finding clothes that fit. I start seeing doctors because

I can't control my weight, and they think I might have diabetes. I can't sleep, spending hours every night second-guessing my actions and questioning where everything went wrong. I start to feel numb inside. I am holding it together for my kids, for my employees, for my company. But I am not sure if I am holding onto anything for myself.

I think we made a big mistake by not sitting down and discussing the divorce with our kids. As a result, my husband told Ryan and Erica things that were untrue. When our son returned home from college for winter break, my husband was sleeping in the guest room. He told Ryan that I was the one breaking up the family. I never explained to our children why we were getting divorced, for the simple reason that I didn't want to tell them things a child should never have to hear about a parent. But that meant I gave them no reasons at all. Outwardly, my husband and I must have seemed happy enough, even to our kids. We didn't fight where anyone could hear us. No wonder they were confused—they never saw it coming.

I thought I was handling the stresses of divorce pretty well. But the effect it was having on me was obvious to everyone else. I went all the way down to a size zero, and then even that was too big. People actually asked me if I had an eating disorder—I was shocked that anyone would come right out with such a question. But maybe they saw that I was in serious trouble and feared that I was unaware of just how bad I looked.

Meanwhile, I was doing everything I could just to get through the day. I started to dread waking up in the morning, not knowing what horrible thing was awaiting me. I held my breath every time my lawyer sent an email, because it usually meant more bad news—some scary new discovery, another unreasonable demand. I especially hate Friday afternoons, because that's when my husband's attorney would invariably send an email that would ruin my weekend. I actually stopped looking at email on Friday afternoons; whatever correspondence they sent could wait until Monday.

Through it all, I never wavered, never considered staying married because I knew things wouldn't change. But the thought of paying alimony for the rest of my life, and providing everything single-handedly for myself and my kids, was more than I could take. At the same time, I had no way out. I felt simultaneously paralyzed and trapped.

I tried to numb my pain by focusing on things that would be good for me. I took up kickboxing and started doing it three times a week. Before long, I broke my wrist. I seemed to be getting hurt a lot then. One day, my daughter told me I should quit, because I was too fragile. She was right. I could barely manage getting through a day. I tried meditation. But it's hard for me to stop my mind from racing. I slept horribly during that period, and when I woke up in the middle of the night, I would lie awake for hours, panicked. Meditation didn't help.

One day, I step into my closet before work to pick out an outfit. My mind is racing. My lawyer has just been in touch with the latest crazy demand from my ex-husband's legal team. I haven't had a good night's sleep in some time, and I have a huge list of things to do today. As I look through the hangers, trying to make a simple decision about what to wear, my mind goes totally blank.

Suddenly, I can't stand. My legs are shaking and my hands tremble. I take a deep breath and sit down on the closet floor. Leaning back against the wall, I begin to sob uncontrollably.

I can't do this. I am worn out. I don't even care.

Minutes go by this way. I'm weeping and gasping for air. No one can help me now. That thought begins to calm me down. The sobbing slows, and I'm beginning to breathe normally. I realize that nobody is going to save me from this closet floor. No one is going to make my divorce any easier. No one is going to run my business for me. No one is going to raise my kids. I am truly all that I have, and I have to keep going. If I don't get up and fight, then I'll lose everything.

That thought sits me upright. I brush the tears from my face. I go to a mirror and see myself, red-nosed and puffy-eyed. But I know something has changed.

I get dressed, start my car, and head to work. Still recovering from my closet meltdown, feeling a storm of emotions, I pull into a gas station. In New Jersey, self-service pumps don't exist, so I just pop open the compartment door, tell the attendant to fill it up, and go back to my whirlwind of thoughts about how I'll manage everything. I am still totally immersed in my head when I turn on the car and pull away into my future.

Then I notice that everyone is waving at me. I look in the mirror and see the hose from the gas pump dangling from my car.

Mortified, I turn back.

I begin tearing through my purse to find my insurance card so I can take responsibility for damages to the pump. The attendant comes over and I lower the window.

"I am *so* sorry," I say. "Hang on a second while I find my card."

"Just pull up to the gas pump, ma'am," he says. "Let me finish filling your car. It looks like you're having a really bad day."

Now I'm really in shock. I start the car and do as he says. I'm taking a few deep breaths as he removes the hose from my tank and inserts a working one.

As the tank fills he comes back to my window and says, "Don't worry about the insurance cards. You didn't do any damage. You are not the first one to drive away from the gas station with the pump still in the car. These are breakaway pumps, they're easy to fix."

I look at him and smile. This is maybe *the* most

ridiculous situation I've ever been in. I really *did* just drive off with a gas pump connected to my car. But it was also maybe the single best thing that happened to me during that terrible time of my life. It reminded me that there are kind people in the world and that sometimes I will encounter one when I need it most. Just because I'd made a dumb mistake doesn't mean my day had to be ruined or that my error couldn't be forgiven.

In one morning, I had a total emotional breakdown on the floor of my closet and one of the funniest moments of my whole life. Somehow, that gave me the hope and the wisdom to go on, despite all the conflict with my ex-husband.

As the attendant hands me my credit card and receipt, he has one last gift to offer.

"I think you should wipe the day clean and start over," he says.

I couldn't agree with him more.

I always thought we were the "happy little family." We looked so great from the outside, I felt, like we "had it all." But truthfully, we did not. I even lost friends who took their time deciding which side to support. I remember one calling and saying, "Even though your ex is hanging out with us, I want you to know we still love you and want to hear your side." I asked him, "Why is that important?" He said, "Well, there's always two sides, we heard his but now we want to hear yours." I told them the details of my failed marriage should not matter, and if he and his wife were my friends, they should realize that.

I let them go. They weren't the only ones.

I felt both excitement and fear regarding the business. At last, I was completely my own, with no input from my ex on how to run the company I had started. That was liberating. But I knew that if I failed, I would have no one to support me and my children—no one to pick up the pieces. If anything happened to Elite, we would have been devastated, financially. Not just my family but also the families of all my employees. What an awesome responsibility. When you own a company, people think you can do whatever you want with it and answer to no one but yourself. The truth is that you answer to *every-one*—your employees, clients, creditors, the bank, suppliers, vendors, on and on.

Still, with all that on my shoulders, I felt renewed. Excited. It was all up to me, and I knew I could make it work. I had a big vision and there was no one to squash my goals. At last—having weathered a bad marriage, a divorce, a sick child—I was free to give my all. I was ready.

CHERYL'S TIP FOR SUCCESS:
Take Care of Yourself First

If you are exhausted, unhealthy, unfocused, or inactive, it will be much harder to live and act in the here and now. I am a huge advocate for taking time to meditate, finding the right way of eating for you, and getting regular exercise and sleep. I now know I can't run myself ragged for weeks and function at my peak—even if I wanted to. I make sure to give myself down time and keep healthy habits so I can be ready to get past the next obstacle that comes my way. For me, laughter helped a lot, even when things weren't really very funny. My divorce was horrible, and yet, when I would pour my heart out to my closest friends, we always found something to crack us up.

But when you need to go in the opposite direction, feel free to go there. My meltdown came at a point where I had no words left to express the overwhelming emotions I was feeling. Sometimes only a total surrender can provide the release we need.

CHAPTER 7

Moving On

After a long, anxious day at the office, I drive home, turn the key, step inside, and take a deep breath. I let my briefcase fall to the floor and hang my jacket in a closet.

Then I take it all in. This home, once shared with my ex, is now mine alone. A few hours ago, I finalized the new mortgage in my name only. After months of untangling our finances, feeling like my life was in utter chaos and at a total standstill, I now own this place. I still can't believe I got approved for the loan. I was panicked that I wouldn't qualify on my own. But the bank gave it to me without much hassle. More unnecessary worry. I only wish the divorce could be completely over, too. My ex has evaded a final settlement a few times and delayed my mortgage closing for several weeks.

I'm through letting this nonsense hurt me. I am my own woman now, and I am taking my life back.

I've really attempted to make this house all mine. I needed to change things after all that's happened in here over the past few years. We bought it together after deciding that a move to Florida wouldn't be good for us. This is also where we decided to divorce after an awful fight. We continued living here together even after we were separated. It's been a roller coaster ride in this place, but that's over.

One easy way for me to take my life back is to focus on little things that can add up to something big. I decided to paint the walls different colors and decorate each room to my taste. This was harder than I expected because I had relied for so long on my husband's opinions before I'd make a decision. With the help of magazines and HGTV, I realized I had an entirely different vision of what my house should look like. It's now a symbol of how I rebuilt my life, on my terms. I'm no longer seeking somebody else's opinions. I'm comfortable relying on my own.

I take off my high heels, walk upstairs to Erica's room to say hello, then head to my bedroom to change into comfy clothes. I spend the evening cooking, curling up in front of my favorite TV shows, and falling asleep with a sense of inner peace. I am slowly breaking away from the chaos that surrounded me for so long. And it feels so good.

My panic attack in my bedroom closet months ago signaled to me that I needed to change direction and pull myself out of the paralysis that my divorce had created. I called my mother just hours after I pulled myself up from the closet floor to tell her my newfound resolve.

"Mom, I just can't live like this any longer," I said. "I need to be my own person again. I have to stop being controlled by these divorce proceedings. He cannot control my happiness."

My mom stayed silent for a few seconds to make sure I was done talking. Finally, she spoke.

"Cheryl, I am so proud of you and so happy to hear this," she said. "You can have a happy life. But it's going to take work." She wasn't saying anything I didn't already know, but it was a huge relief to hear her say it.

Starting that day, I resolved to pick myself up and make life happen again. One defining moment occurred when I told my ex-husband to stop contacting me directly about anything beyond Erica's care. He had been texting and sending me not-so-nice messages and letters for quite a while, and they were getting me down. I have to admit that I got my message across in a pretty blunt way—I really felt the need to throw the ball back at him. I would not respond to this any longer, I said. From now on he couldn't control me. Anything unrelated to Erica had to go through our attorneys. It took him a while to catch up with my new boundaries, but after a few weeks of no replies, he stopped texting me. I didn't miss this.

I had never lived on my own, so being a forty-year-old woman ready to take her life back took some figuring out. I had spent half of my years on Earth being a wife and a mother. Before that I was a child living under my parents' roof. I didn't really know what *I* liked to do, or what it meant to exist and have fun without my family by my side. My life as entrepreneur and CEO of Elite had consumed every minute that I wasn't with my husband and children.

Now, I'm a single woman with a son in college in Florida and a teenage daughter who doesn't want to spend all her time with her mother. It feels strange.

The first thing that becomes clear is that my former social life has changed forever. The people with whom I spent so many hours while we raised our kids are no longer in my life. The friends my ex-husband and I shared were mostly couples. Everything we did together was meant for twosomes. Meeting for drinks or dinners, or hosting parties at home to watch football on TV—you'd think a single woman could take part in all that, but it doesn't work that way. We weren't individuals—we were couples. At our get-togethers, the men would gather and we women did the same, to chat about work and home and kids and our latest vacations.

Suddenly, these gatherings weren't so much fun for me. I felt awkward standing in the kitchen with the women while they discussed their husbands, or couple plans, and then asked me—a little too gently—about how my divorced life was going. They tried to come across as empathetic, but I could tell that my situation made them sad and uncomfortable. I felt defensive and sensitive during these gatherings, like my life was over.

But away from these social events, I felt just the opposite. I was suddenly carefree and fun-loving among my new friends. Those couple parties just reminded me of my past. The last thing I wanted to remember.

I figured out that I needed to find some new friends while also nurturing relationships that were still important to me. I also had to learn how to have fun. My friend Jill and my sister Vicki were my rocks as I reinvented myself. My sister always listens to me, and I know I can trust her opinions. She won't sugarcoat advice, and she's a very logical thinker. Jill supports me every step of the way and is always willing to pick up the phone when I call. And my new girlfriends and I get together to have fun as single women. We regularly meet at restaurants to laugh and share stories about our new lives.

I slowly begin to regain the weight I shed during my divorce. Better to lose weight than to gain it, you might think, but it got to where my doctor was concerned. He actually insisted I come in periodically for weight checks. I had to constantly get my clothes taken in to keep me looking professional. The tailor at one point asked why I kept buying clothes that were too big. Thankfully, as I gained more control of my life, I was able to fix my eating habits and return to my natural size.

As time goes by, I get more in touch with what it feels like to live again. I am definitely not ready to date seriously, but I don't need a partner to experience life at the fullest. I rent a condo in Miami for a week and invite my son to join me. We go out to enjoy the nightlife and really have a great time. Despite the fact that I'm with my adult son, I immediately feel twenty years younger. We meet all sorts of interesting people, try new restaurants, and even dance at the clubs. My constant smiling and laughing says it all: Not only have I left the bad days of my divorce hundreds of miles away, but the acrimony and trauma are gone, too. As I pack my bags and head to the airport for the flight back to Delaware, I'm still buzzed with the positive energy from the trip. It just affirms to me that I was right to move on from misery and frustration. I head back home in a great state of mind. I have plenty more life to live.

∞

I finally receive my divorce decree. It's been two years since my husband and I decided to separate. With the official document in hand, I leave the courtroom with mixed emotions. I feel relief, sadness, gratitude, and frustration, all at the same time.

The decree represents closure and lifts a huge burden off my shoulders. The divorce has dominated two years of my life and has taken me places I never expected to be, like the floor of my closet. I've spent thousands of dollars on lawyers' fees in order to bicker with my ex about every possible aspect of our marriage and finances. I am excited to free my time and energy with this final step.

But I also reflect on my marriage and feel sadness and sorrow at the end of such a long relationship. The twenty-three-year bond that he and I shared is now over. It's history. At one point we did love each other. We met as children and grew up together. We invested in our futures and supported each other in our twenties and thirties. We created a family and dreamed big together. We dealt with difficult situations as parents, like getting Erica the care she needed. We embraced the hopes and dreams of our kids and did what we could to help them achieve what they wanted. I don't regret our years together and I am forever grateful for our children.

I'm also frustrated. Concluding this split has stretched me financially and I'll feel it for years to come. The terms we finally agreed to at the end of negotiations nearly impoverished me. I agreed to pay my ex alimony for the rest of my life, in addition to buying him out of the house we shared. He was able to move on to a new life, while I am stuck bankrolling him for the rest of our days. I can't even wrap my head around the total long-term financial burden of the divorce, but I am relieved to stop paying lawyers.

When I pull up to my house on the day of the divorce decree, I walk through the door wiping tears from my eyes. This is a far different, sadder day than the one when I closed on my new mortgage.

Thankfully, I don't enter an empty house. I walk in and smell home cooking, and see my friend Jill and her boyfriend, Ken. They greet me in the dining room with glasses of wine and a delicious dinner. We sit together for most of the night, finding things to laugh about. We share some serious moments, too.

The most important thing is that rather than being alone on this sorrowful day, I can share it with some amazing people who have stuck by me for so many years. When I finally head to bed that night, I know it's time to let the past go and figure out what I want to accomplish and achieve in the here and now.

CHERYL'S TIP FOR SUCCESS:
Trust Is Key

The only reason I came out of my divorce okay was because I had people I could trust. Not only did I require support in my personal life, I also needed my crew at Elite to make sure the company didn't fall apart while I was distracted. The true friendships I had with my sister Vicki and Jill were also crucial to helping me pick up the pieces. My divorce shook me of self-confidence to the point where I barely recognized myself. I needed honest feedback to get me through that troubled time. Without trusted friendships, I have no idea what would have happened to me. I've often heard that trust takes years to build and seconds to break. Take a good look at who you let into your life, and make sure they have your back.

CHAPTER 8

A Time to Be Clear

It's been months since I've been able to give Elite the attention it deserves. Thankfully, my great staff has kept things afloat while my mind was elsewhere. My company has remained the same size for a few years now. At this point we have business in several mid-Atlantic states and about 100 employees. I am still running it with the values-driven mindset I had in the early days, and the loyalty of my staff showed when I was too distracted to pull my own weight. We got a bit of new business from referrals, but I haven't been out there selling our services like in the past.

I am hungry for faster growth and with good reason: I'm supporting two children, one of whom is in college, the other soon to be. And I'm paying alimony. I want to provide my kids with a comfortable life. I also want to hire more employees and reward those already on the payroll. I can't afford to be satisfied with the status quo.

My resolve has some barriers, though. My business development staffer has just given notice and is moving to Atlanta. I'm feeling rusty and a little off my selling game, and think maybe it's time to rethink my approach. I need to find someone to fill my business development needs, and the person can't just be anyone off the street.

I begin to look for a new person in a pretty casual way. I plan to network with my clients before even considering writing a job description and posting the opening. An advantage of operating out of Delaware is that it is a small, tight-knit business community, full of people who are ambitious and committed to the good of the state. Wilmington itself is a vibrant business hub despite its small size. When I first started working there, most businesses were committed to dealing with other local firms, but that has evolved over time as technology allows access to clients and opportunities in other places. Nonetheless, the city is home to many major credit card companies and banks, law offices, and insurers. All of which require cleaning services.

I am looking for a person who will work

alongside me and respect my approach. I've been a woman entrepreneur for two decades now and I don't need someone to come in and challenge my opinions or vision. Of course, I'm looking for someone who will speak up if I seem to be headed in a wrong direction. But I don't want a battle for control. I've definitely had enough of that in my life already!

A client of mine, the president of a construction and development company, suggests I talk to his cousin, who is between jobs. Cousin Hank worked in New York, in private equity, when the economy took a dive and his company closed. He moved back to Wilmington to pursue work near his family —his father's side has been in Delaware politics for many generations and his mother's family has in construction and development since the early 1900s. That alone speaks volumes to me.

Hank and I schedule lunch together at a restaurant in Wilmington. I am not about to offer him any kind of job, knowing that his salary expectations after a decade in banking will be too high for me to meet. But we plan to get together anyway—it's always helpful to know someone with deep ties in Delaware.

Over our two-hour lunch, Hank and I put everything on the table. I am instantly charmed by his personality. He is approachable and charismatic as well as an excellent listener. I tell him Elite's story and my own. I discuss beginning the business, growing it, and overcoming obstacles like Erica's medical needs and the end of my marriage. I emphasize my great team and the challenges I face as a woman CEO in the cleaning and building services industry. Hank tells me his work history, including his time as a small business owner, his experience with his family's company, and his recent detour after the economy's meltdown. He opens up about his wife and kids—he's been married for a long time, and they raised a son and a daughter. We laugh over stories about parenting boys and girls.

Then we start brainstorming about what's next for my company. He talks about what I might need to grow Elite. His perspective opens my eyes to all that I'll have to do if I want to expand, and I realize that I'll need someone with a lot of talent and experience to help make this happen. Neither one of us holds back, and by the end of lunch we're both pretty excited about the future.

As much as I enjoy the conversation, I still know that I can't offer Hank a job. At the same time, I feel that I can't afford to pass up the opportunity to work with him. He is also intrigued and feels excited by the possibility of helping me achieve great things at Elite.

"Listen, Hank," I say. "I really like you and think you have unmatched talents to offer Elite. You could be the magic ticket to help us soar to new heights. But there is no way I can pay you like an executive banker in New York. I can't match the salary now, but I really think we can move to a new level and that I can make up your sacrifices today if you hang in there with me for the next few years."

My offer isn't in contract form and doesn't guarantee much more than a stable job with a modest paycheck. But Hank accepts my proposal anyway. He takes the leap of faith and comes aboard, knowing that I'll fulfill my promises to him over the next several years. We shake hands and get to work.

I make this offer without stepping back and thinking about what I am doing, but only because we click with no effort at all. Sometimes in life it's important to throw slow and steady out the window, and during this lunch I realize that I need

Hank at Elite. I wasn't interested in checking out his references or talking to others about him. After all, I had been in business for twenty years and had learned a thing or two about identifying talent.

Ever since that day, I am constantly reminded of what a good decision I made. Hank is well-known in the Delaware business community. Every time he and I are out together, someone comes over to chat with him. He always remembers small details about people's lives, like their children's names or their mother's recent illness. No one has ever had a bad thing to say about him. And he brought an excitement to the business. He is as driven as I am. I need a co-pilot, someone who was encouraging and also knew more about business than I did. He had unbelievable connections, and to this day I've never met anyone who doesn't like and respect him. I knew that with Hank by my side that this company was going places. I was beyond excited.

One year after Hank comes on board, Elite already looks quite a bit different. I am still uphold-ing my original values of hard work and excellent customer service, and we're growing at a faster rate than we imagined. Our success is in large part due to Hank's insight. He realizes quickly that I am the key to attracting new clients. He can strategize about how to raise capital, hire staff, and identify potential new clients, but he recognizes my strengths on the sales side.

My love of getting out there and selling is what keeps me going year after year. I love meeting new people, shaking their hands, connecting with them, and showing them what Elite can do. I did it with my first bosses, Jerry and Bill, when I persuaded them to let me clean their office building. No matter how shaky I've been in my personal life, I have never been too nervous to go door to door to find business or pitch a big client who seemed out of my league. Doing deals makes me feel empowered and emboldened. I don't let fear hold me back. It transforms me into a person who is laser-focused on job one: signing new clients.

A few of the reasons I am so motivated to sell Elite's services is because I know we're the best and I thrive on building relationships so we can prove it. By this point in time, Elite is fulfilling many different types of services, but I know that no matter what we are doing for clients—whether cleaning a medical center, providing window cleanings for a high-rise building, or caring for a corporate chain's floors—they can expect excellent service. I make sure that our rates are competitive but not too low. I am very much against low-balling customers because I don't think it's a good business model and it undercuts the services we can provide. Cheapest is not always best, I often say to clients and staff. My philosophy is that Elite can provide good quality for a reasonable price. It's what keeps the business sustainable, pays the bills, and compensates the staff with fair and competitive wages.

Elite is able to keep growing because of loyal clients who understand our commitment to excellence and our willingness to acknowledge and fix mistakes. I am never hesitant to own up to an oversight. My staff members are human and things can go wrong. To me, it is more important to take responsibility for an error, remedy it immediately, and make sure it doesn't happen again.

My drive to grow Elite propels me into a much healthier mindset. I might be giving everything to the business, but I am seeing huge gains with each passing month because of my efforts. My momentum is pulling me out of a post-divorce funk. I no longer have the demands of being a mother to young children, so I have many more hours available to work. Sales pitches call me out of the office frequently, but it doesn't stop me from keeping regular hours at Elite's headquarters.

I want to know my employees on personal terms. To me, my compassion toward them is a strength, something that I can bring as a female entrepreneur. I have raised two children while working and know the frequent demands of home life. I want my employees to take vacations, attend their children's activities, and utilize other benefits. I feel like providing a good work-home life balance for my staff will result in a positive culture above and beyond work. Hank sometimes grumbles about my too-lenient stance on certain employee policies, but I really believe that creating a healthy environment sets Elite apart from other businesses in the industry and has contributed to our solid reputation.

It is important to me that my employees not only feel valued at Elite but that they also feel good when they come to work each day. I make sure that our headquarters are comfortable and attractive so the people who spend forty hours a week there feel at ease. I make sure my traditional decorating tastes come across as warm and friendly. I am not going for a stodgy, highfalutin' look in our line of work! I choose warm colors with bright white trim, good-quality carpet and hardwood floors, and make sure our lunchroom and conference room are appropriately furnished. Most people have individual offices, but we keep the operations teams in the center of the space. We call it "the bullpen." It's important that members of our operations team can interact with each other throughout the day because their paths constantly cross. Our offices need to foster collaboration because we really can't get the job done without working as a team.

As the company grows, I have to think of new ways to appreciate the staff. We're now too big to run an employee award system, with 750 workers in several states. We even opened an office in Florida to meet our expanding needs. So I make sure we find small ways to recognize people. I offer free lunch on Thursdays because it's the day we schedule quite a few meetings. This way everyone can relax a bit while we strategize and problem-solve together in the conference room.

Promoting a friendly work environment means more than just providing a nice office and paying for lunch once a week, though. I am committed to setting an example for the staff of how to communicate with each other. I firmly believe that how top-level workers interact with each other has a tremendous impact throughout the workplace. When Hank came on board, we were all made aware that our tone with each other sets a company-wide standard. We work together effortlessly and respectfully. We keep our focus on the vision and do not compete with one another to fulfill goals along the way. It is a huge relief and a motivator to work with someone so agreeable and knowledgeable.

After a few years of working alongside Hank, I realize I have never trusted a colleague more. When he and I had that first lunch, I was still struggling to gain back the self-confidence shattered by the disaster of my personal life. Working alongside someone so capable has made a huge difference in how I approach my job. I don't have to scrutinize every part of the business as I had done before. I know Hank can make the right decisions on many issues without my meddling. This helps me focus on growing our client list.

Hank believes in me, too, but he knows that I am capable of more. I sense that he sees some of the damage that I experienced following the years of my crumbling marriage. He also knows I feel tremendous responsibility to be a stable force for my children and my team, which takes a lot of energy. I am not able to give myself time or space to grow and reflect. I don't invest in personal and professional development opportunities. I just respond to the daily pressure to get out there and close deals and keep the work and the money coming in.

In my early days at Elite, I worked like I had nothing to lose. I stuck my neck out when I started cleaning Bill and Jerry's building in the 1980s, motivated to earn more than my secretary job could offer. I left that steady position not long after I began cleaning the office building because I knew I would make something of the opportunity. As a twenty-something, I had the fire to make good things happen in my life, even with a young child and barely any savings. Methodically, I built my business brick by brick, full of the self-confidence to make it happen.

It was never easy, but I never backed away from the challenge in those younger days.

Two decades later, though, I have changed. I am grateful that my early hard work has built a stable business, but my approach to work and life is very different now. Over the years, I have become more of a passive observer of my own life, as a way of surviving the challenges at home. I have grown comfortable with my upper-middle-class lifestyle and do not find reasons to challenge that identity, only to persevere. I work hard, but I am not in a transformative or empowered space. I keep my outlook pretty simple. I want to grow Elite because I love selling our services to people, knowing how well we do our job, and also because it will help me pay my bills. I see very little in my own value beyond running a business in the cleaning services industry.

But Hank has a plan to push me in a new direction. He wants me to embrace my successes and become more visible. To him, this is important for the company's growth and also for my identity. He knows I need guidance—and not just from him. One day, Hank arranges for me to meet with Sara Canuso, a coach for professional women at the top of their game. Sara has worked in Philadelphia for many years and runs her own successful business that helps women achieve the most from their professional and personal lives. Hank's wife reached out to Sara first, thinking she would be the right person to help me see beyond the immediate needs of Elite and shape me into a visionary leader and entrepreneur.

I'm not convinced. I am growing Elite just as Hank and I had planned, and I don't see anything wrong with my approach. I'm not looking to put anything more on my plate.

Still, I agree to meet Sara and get to know her. I am impressed by her poise, influence, and confidence. She has a huge network of female entrepreneurs. I can relate to her professional story, as she has worked tirelessly in the corporate world from the bottom up and transitioned to starting her own company several years ago. She's aware of the challenges of being a female entrepreneur and has experience guiding women to new heights. I feel at ease when I talk with Sara—it's the same feeling I had during my first lunch with Hank.

As Sara opens up about her life, I do, too. I talk about my achievements at Elite as well as my personal triumphs and tragedies. I tell her about my children and the many obstacles my daughter has faced during her life. I share some of the details of my marriage and the long, brutal process of ending it.

It doesn't take long for Sara to size me up. She says my story is remarkable and that I am clearly a very capable chief executive. She is amazed at how I put my life together after such a destructive divorce. But she also points out that I am holding myself back. She sees how I make decisions about my current life always looking over my shoulder, waiting for the next thing to explode. My life as an adult has not always been easy, and I have grown accustomed to not getting too comfortable for too long, always waiting for the next crisis.

Sara calls me out on that. Appreciating her candor, I decide to take the leap and let her coach me.

CHERYL'S TIP FOR SUCCESS:
Expand Your Circle

Though I had twenty years of work experience under my belt and my business was in good shape, I decided to let new people into my life to help me grow. It caught me off guard because I had made it through so many years of challenge without outside help. But I reached a place where I needed new people to reinvigorate me and to help me see what I could not. Hank was a game changer as I refocused and considered the future of the business. He brought not only years of work experience to the table but also a friendly and compassionate demeanor. Sara was someone who I needed desperately in my life even though I resisted it at first. I'd had the support of friends and family who would side with me no matter what I did. Sara and Hank would point out where I needed work. Over time, this helped me become more introspective and see things that I needed to change.

CHAPTER 9

Onward and Upward

"Cheryl, it's time you embraced who you are and let the world see it," Sara says to me over dinner one night. "You are still driving the same old beat-up SUV that you drove ten years ago, and your wardrobe could use some help."

I look at her, a little shocked. I'm still getting used to being somebody's project. I know I am paying her to help me achieve some professional breakthroughs, but I'm not accustomed to being analyzed quite so intimately.

"I guess I could," I say. "It's just that I don't want to spend a lot of money on myself right now. I've got the kids and the alimony. I don't want to be too showy either."

"But you are the chief executive of a very successful business," Sara replies. "You've got to be willing to share your success on the outside.

Potential clients are sizing you up before you've even spoken to them. You've got to look the part."

She's right. I know it. It's been years since I bought much of anything for myself. I've been replenishing my savings after paying off lawyers and getting used to my new monthly budget, which includes a hefty payment to my ex.

"And it's not just your outward appearance that is holding you back," Sara goes on. "You aren't out at enough events, talking to the right people. At this stage of your career, you should be connecting with more high-level entrepreneurs and executives. Especially if you want your company to grow."

This feedback is even harder to take. I'm working sixty-hour-plus weeks at Elite and she doesn't think I'm doing enough?

"But how am I supposed to get new clients if I'm not focusing everything I have on Elite?" I ask, as politely as possible.

"Cheryl, you are doing what you need to do to keep Elite at the level it is. But I know you and Hank want more for this company. You have to elevate yourself and new business will come—on a whole different level than what you currently have. You need to think bigger. You'll get into more conversations with more important people if you widen your net."

I pick at my salad and listen to Sara say all the right things, even if I don't want to hear them. There are reasons that I hold back on my response, and I don't know if I can verbalize my fears.

"I'll think about it," I say.

I want to tell Sara why I'm timid and afraid to raise my business profile, but I am so paralyzed by fear that I don't even know how to begin. I have been working very hard at Elite to get back on track, and Hank and I have so many great ideas and plans. But I am hesitant to pull the trigger because fear sits on my shoulder and whispers in my ear every time I think about doing something that might get the attention of my ex-husband.

I continue to make support payments in addition to paying him half of the equity in our house, since I kept it. I also had to give him half of what the furnishings were worth. And I had to buy him out of Elite—I owed him half the value of the company, even though he wasn't a legal partner. This obligation required expert consultants to determine how much my company was worth. When that number came in, I had to figure out how I could give him half of it plus everything else I had to hand over without losing my business or my home. My divorce has devastating financial consequences.

Once my divorce became final, my torture still didn't come to an end. According to our agreement, I was also going to have to pay permanent alimony, meaning that for the rest of my life I'd be supporting my ex-husband. New Jersey was one of the last states still to allow that arrangement. I had to maintain him in his accustomed lifestyle—which *I* had provided while we were married—even after the marriage was over.

Was I bitter? Every time I had to sign another check for him, I relived the whole experience in my mind, which only made me more furious. Why should I have to struggle to keep him in a lifestyle that I could no longer afford for myself? I was barely surviving under the weight of college tuition, medical bills, and a home to support.

Month after month I make my alimony payments, always worrying that somehow I will still owe even more. I am afraid to put Elite or myself in the spotlight because I fear my ex will go to court and demand that I pay extra. I drive an old SUV because I don't want him to think I can afford something nicer. I don't follow up on Hank's ideas because if I do sign a big client, my ex might come knocking. So, Sara's advice that I up my game and bring new business to Elite is basically dead on arrival. I don't want more attention because I don't want to be squeezed for my monetary value. I am tired and scared of what could happen.

I still get mad thinking about it. I had to give him half the equity in the house, which was fair, half the contents of the house, which was fair, but then I had to give him half the value of my company and permanent alimony. Years later, New Jersey's governor changed this law, however, it did not change my situation, but there were some stipulations written in so that people did not co-habitate and still get alimony. He began living with someone on and off. I gathered enough information that allowed me to challenge co-habitation and eventually settle with a mediator for alimony to end. A weight lifted off my shoulders and allowed me to be free at last.

&

Despite all that, Sara convinces me to appear on something called Executive Leadership Radio to share my perspective as a chief executive officer. I have five to ten minutes to talk about what I do and how I lead my company. I try to swallow my fears and get through the interview. I am not the only one appearing on the show that day. I listen to other business leaders talk about their work, and an attorney's segment catches my attention. Mathieu Shapiro talks about how he is a divorce attorney for businesses. He helps companies split up if the partners or owners decide to part ways. This topic intrigues me because of my own recent experiences dividing assets.

A few days after the show, I am still thinking about what he said and decide to call him. We chat for a few minutes before I have the courage to delve into my real reason for getting in touch.

"Mathieu," I say, "have you ever dealt with personal divorces? I am paying permanent alimony to my ex-husband, and I want to know if I will have to keep this up forever and whether he can come back and demand more from me. It's such a stressor in my life, and I feel like I can't even provide myself the lifestyle I would like and could pay for without these financial requirements."

All my worries spill out to this stranger. I've spoken all the thoughts that nag at me on a daily basis, the ones that have been holding me and my company back for so long.

"Cheryl," he says, "this is really not my line of work, but I have a great recommendation for a personal attorney that can give you advice on how to handle it."

That attorney ends up being a huge life-changer for me. She sits me down and we go through my financial obligations.

"Cheryl," she says, "the terms you agreed to a few years ago will stay the same over time. Your ex-husband received half the value of the company during your marriage. He has no say in what the company does now, so you are under no obligation to pay him more."

She gives me the reality check that I need. She also insists that I challenge the permanent alimony judgment, especially now that my husband is supposedly seeing a woman.

I'm reluctant to do that, just because I dread going back to court and reliving the conflict yet again. But the time finally comes for me to challenge my obligation. It has become clear to me that I am being taken advantage of, and New Jersey's law change pushes me over the edge. My attorney explains that a court would view my ex's new relationship as negating our settlement. I decide it's finally time to free myself, even if it means going back into the world of attorneys, judges, and arguments about money. I think to myself, "Here we go again."

First, I had to prove that my ex and his girlfriend shared a home. Easier said than done, since he knew that it could cost him his alimony payments. I had to establish proof of co-habitation and that they presented themselves in public as a couple. Then they split up, which of course put a freeze on my plan. Finally, after about a year and a half of gathering information, we got proof that they lived together (or near enough).

The court battle is much like my divorce, except that now it's just about money, and I don't feel emotionally entangled in the fight. The children come up again, even though Ryan is grown and married and Erica is nearing the end of her college education. My husband fights my challenge to the alimony by providing bank statements and other documents, but ultimately the case goes to mediation.

The mediator listens to our stories. When it's my turn to speak, I suggest that my ex and I come to an immediate agreement to terminate alimony and forgive back payments owed to me for higher education and hospital bills. Though the mediator is unable to make a binding decision like a judge would, he tells my husband that settling for my offer is in his best interest.

Even with that, I had to offer my ex a lump sum payoff. I wrote one last check and with that, alimony was over and my freedom and peace of mind were back to where I needed it to be.

But what an ordeal!

My business helped me get through that period in an unexpected way. It showed me how important it is to surround yourself with the right people. Hank and the rest of our staffers were all on my side. They liked me and respected me. They treated me the way I had always wanted to be treated. At some point, I realized how much that matters—you have to carefully choose the people you spend your time with. They have to be on your side. If not, they'll drag you down.

Of course, you also have to be on their side. It's a two-way street. When it works that way, everybody is lifted up. We all feel better about ourselves. Doesn't matter what you're talking about—a company, a marriage, a family, a team, a group of friends. If you're spending time with the wrong people, nothing will go right.

After working with Sara for a while, I decide to hire her away from her booming consulting business. This move doesn't come completely out of the blue. It's just like the moment I realized I needed Hank on board. I feel like I'm finally reaching my own untapped potential, and I don't want to lose this momentum. It takes a bit of persuasion, but I finally present Sara with a deal she can't refuse.

Now Hank and Sara are both in my ear about getting my name out beyond the Mid-Atlantic area. Hank wants the business to grow regionally and then nationally. Sara wants me to advocate for other women who have faced the same obstacles that I have. She believes in me and says that I can use my voice to connect to others who are struggling. I doubt that, but Sara is an optimistic force of nature.

She says she wants me to start giving speeches.

"One day I will," I promise. But it isn't something I'm looking forward to.

Not long after, I'm away from the office on business when Sara calls to say she just booked me as the keynote speaker at an event called the New Jersey Annual Women's Conference.

"Sara," I tell her, exasperated, "I said I would try speaking in public *one day*, not right away!"

"There's no such thing as one day," she replies. "One day is going to be here in exactly two months. We have to get ready."

I am terrified for two solid months. This is a big deal, with an audience of 350 women. The night before my speech, I go to bed but can't sleep. I read my notes again and again and deliver my talk to the ceiling.

In the morning a car arrives to take me to the event, and when I get there I find a large photo of me in the lobby, announcing that I will be making the keynote address.

I am seated at the head table for lunch. I can't eat a bite. Instead, I quietly tremble the entire time.

I am so scared that I will disappoint Sara and all the other women in the room.

Someone standing at the lectern reads my bio, and then I hear my name. As I stand, Sara whispers to me, "Just speak from your heart."

That calms me down. I know my story well. If I forget something, nobody in the room will know.

I'm pretty sure my voice is shaking as I begin to speak. Sara says she couldn't tell and neither could anyone else. I lay out my entire life for the audience. It's not a pep talk or an inspirational speech, but it's the only story I know. Sara and I debated what to put into it, and she convinced me that I needed to tell it with no filters. I give up the whole truth about my marriage and my meltdown and all the rest. I tell how it felt to hit rock bottom, what it's like to be afraid and exhausted but knowing you have no choice but to keep going. I share the funny stories, too, like driving away from the gas pump a little too soon, and running over the same deer twice: once by accident and a second time when I went back to see if it was okay.

When I finish, the room explodes in applause. Or at least it feels that way to me. Someone brings me a bouquet of flowers. As I step down from the stage, I find a line of women waiting to talk to me.

Over and over, I hear the same things:

"I just want you to know, I am going through a divorce and found your words to be so inspiring. Thank you for being so honest."

"Your experience with your daughter reminds me of my life with my own child."

"I've been in your shoes. The way you tell your story inspires me."

"How did you decide to keep going when life got so hard?"

Many of them have their own stories to tell, about the struggles they're dealing with. Some of them cry. They thank me for not trying to paint a picture that being a woman and a mother starting a business is easy because it definitely is not.

I am beside myself with the response to this presentation. Just hours ago I was a nervous wreck, wondering why I was putting myself through this, and why I always thought I needed to be more and do more. I could have turned this speech down and stayed in the office, plugging away at my to-do list. Now I am seeing firsthand how many women can relate to my story. It's truly transformative.

I have had many other occasions to speak to women's groups since then, annual meetings, associations, and so on. I will say it has gotten easier, but I still get butterflies right before I take the stage. I recently spoke at a conference where I received a standing ovation, and afterward a woman came up and said, "Thank you for keeping it real. I'm so tired of hearing women stand up there speaking with candy canes hanging out of their asses."

I think I know what she meant. She was a single mother with a special-needs child. Her life is hard. I feel like my story gives comfort to women who have dreams for their own careers. They know that they have to do it their way, in their own time. They're not young, single women straight out of college with business degrees or MBAs. Their lives aren't so different from mine. They see how bumpy my road was, and it gives them hope. If I'm helping them, I feel like I'm doing something right.

CHERYL'S TIP FOR SUCCESS:
Rise Up to Challenges

Though I was fearful in the years that followed my divorce, I never stopped seeking answers or finding new ways to approach obstacles in my path. I found professionals who could identify where aspects of my life should change and guide me to face the challenges that came with breaking new ground. I persisted in finding a way to challenge the court-ordered lifetime alimony. I raised my voice in a group of women professionals to tell my story of success and achievement. These events were not easy and did not happen without putting myself out there. I am so fortunate that I found the right people to help me on my journey, and I am grateful that I overcame these obstacles and pushed myself into new places.

CHAPTER 10

Here and Now

It's a new world now that I have no financial obligations to my ex-husband, and children who have grown into adults. For so long, I felt like I was pedaling a bike as fast as I could and never getting ahead. I am finally free to live life on my own terms. There is no way I am going to squander this hard-fought freedom.

I've always made decisions at Elite and at home by staying true to the values I learned as a kid and have refined ever since. I've identified what's important and what should be discarded without a second thought. I use my instincts to make decisions and ensure that I surround myself with my family and my closest friends and coworkers.

Sara and Hank continue to push me to break free of my once-fearful outlook. I am no longer a scared-stiff divorcée. I am a woman running a very successful company, and I deserve more than I used to give myself credit for. They encourage me to embrace these changes and position myself properly to the outside world. I sell my old SUV and upgrade to a new BMW. I buy nice clothes again, befitting a CEO. I'm finally living the lifestyle that I have always deserved.

One of the most delightful developments in my professional and personal life is that my children end up working at the company after college. I am amazed that they are still willing to see me on a daily basis! I know that some kids need to go off and spread their wings—I certainly did when I married young, moved to a new city, and started a family in my early twenties. But my own offspring seem content to stay close to home and work at the family business. We are careful to keep boundaries so our lives don't get *too* emmeshed, which I think is key to sustaining our relationships.

Ryan is now working out of the Delaware office, after spending several years down in Washington, DC and Virginia with some of our construction and data center clients. My daughter, Erica, joins the team after college and is a positive presence in the office, always quick to offer praise. The three of us—Ryan,

Erica, and myself—often have lunch together. I am grateful that we can all work at the same place and still be close despite how often we interact.

Hank, Sara, and I are still hard at work building the brand. We're planning to grow into new states and add to our team over the next few years. I am focused on signing big clients and pushing myself into larger networks. Sara guides me on how I can get there by raising my public profile. She's booked me for so many speaking gigs that I feel completely comfortable in front of an audience, unlike that first experience when I was like a deer in the headlights.

My personal life is blossoming as well. A girl-friend and I went to Cabo San Lucas to celebrate my fiftieth birthday, a big milestone that prompted me to think of my past and my future. She still teases me about our night out at a resort nightclub: We were having a ball, dancing with our fellow vaca-tioners, when a bittersweet moment occurred as I announced, "I am fifty and divorced!" My friends and I have helped each other through the hard times, so it was pure joy to let go and enjoy our-selves in Mexico's tropical paradise.

I am now fortunate to be a grandmother. Ryan has two daughters, and I get to spend regular time with them. They call me "Cece." Life as Cece is so much fun because I get to spoil those girls when I have them over for the night and then send them home sugared up and happy. My oldest granddaughter is eight, and she always knows that we'll make ice cream sundaes with all the fixings—including her favorite, "whippity cream." Ryan will even bring the girls to the office sometimes when we're working late. I love watching him being a doting father.

My daughter recently moved into her own apartment, so I've been adjusting to life as an empty nester. It's a lot quieter at home than it was five or ten years ago. My weekends are now relaxed and carefree; with so much going on at work during the week, I rely on quiet time to slow down and recharge. I enjoy having time for spontaneity, having spent so many years being responsible, attending kid activities and doctor's appointments, and seeing to everyone else first.

Along the way I met a wonderful man named Bob. Hank fixed us up on a blind date and we hit it off from the start. Bob and I started out spending weekends together, then weeknights, too, and after two years of this, he proposed. And I accepted. After the disappointment and drama of my first marriage, this is something I never expected to do again. Finding that right person in your life is worth the wait. Never close yourself off to possibilities.

I am still very close to my family and check in regularly with my parents and sister. My mom and dad continue to model integrity in how they live their lives and are a shining example to my siblings and me. My sister Vicki and I talk on the phone every day. I laugh because she's raising her young kids alongside my grandkids! My brother has two grown sons who I am very close to. We spend holidays together.

Of course, the female relationships in my life are especially valuable to me. I am lucky to have Jill, my sister Vicki, Sara, and several other friends to talk to, on the phone or at dinner. My friend Barbara, who is an excellent listener and dishes out great advice, works at a boutique and helps me dress like the person I want to project to the world. Given that I spent years tailoring too-big clothes to save money, being able to outfit myself appropriately has done wonders to my feelings of self-worth.

I've begun taking care of my body and soul, too. I am very disciplined now about eating healthy, getting the right kind of exercise, and meditating regularly. I avoid relationships that are drama filled or toxic. I am not interested in negativity at this stage in my life. Prioritizing my physical and mental health is something I should have done ages ago, but I am making up for lost time.

My life will always have its ups and downs. The Covid pandemic forced Elite to pivot from simple cleaning to the urgent need for disinfecting. Many of our clients shut their offices down, but new ones came along—essential businesses that had to remain in operation—and this actually increased the demand for our services.

Covid also had a very personal impact on my family. We lost my brother, Jim, in April 2021, at the age of fifty-five, due to cancer and Covid-related pneumonia. As I write this I'm crying at the thought of my poor brother, who had been so happy with where his life was taking him. Losing Jim at such a young age made me realize the value of living each day to its fullest. I miss him every day.

As I enter a new decade and the second half of life, I realize that I'm in a very strong place. Looking back, I see that I have navigated some major peaks and valleys, and spent a lot of time under siege. Of course, I have some regrets, but I am also proud that I raised two great kids, got Erica past her medical hardships, and found myself alive and well after a brutal divorce. Letting go of fear has been critical, and it's transformative to live with my new mindset.

I look forward to what the next years and decades will bring. I hope to connect more with women who have faced their own challenges. There is so much we can learn from each other. As I started out by saying, most of us are climbing a lattice, not a ladder, and life will take us in many directions. I am mindful that my own lattice will lead me along new paths, and I may not always know where I'm going. But I do know where I'm headed. And I'm hopeful that my experiences—positive and negative—will take me there.

My wish for you is that you can say the same.

Acknowledgments

I want to express my heartfelt gratitude to my family and friends who stayed by my side with their love, support, and encouragement.

To Dr. Michael and Diana Peper, my parents: Thank you for a lifetime of love, support, encouragement, and sense of humor. You both have always led by example, teaching us to give our very best toward everything we do in life and to live a life of integrity and compassion for others.

To Jim Peper Sr., my brother, who brought our family laughter and love: You were always encouraging and optimistic and strived to make everyone happy. The day you passed away left a void in my life that will always be there. You are so loved and missed. You are always in my heart.

To my sister, Vicki Conteh, and best friend, Jill Rawls, who together pulled me up when I felt my mind and spirit falling into a place of hopelessness: Thank you for your continued support throughout my life.

To Ryan Ecton and Erica Ecton, my children, who I look upon every day with admiration, love, and excitement: I am so proud of you both.

To Richard and Susie Conway, thank you for holding Elite together and for the support you provided during my divorce. I am forever thankful for your years of dedication and loyalty.

To Hank Winchester III, my company's executive director and my friend: Thank you for helping me see the vision, taking that risk to help me achieve it, and sticking by my side. And, most important, for introducing me to my husband.

To Sara Canuso, my coach and friend: Thank you for helping me regain my confidence and showing me that I am "unstoppable." You continue to be that constant source of encouragement in my life.

To Dr. Bob Olivieri, my husband and my best friend: Thank you for showing me that finding love again was worth the wait. Thank you for always having my back. You are my rock!

About the Author

Cheryl Ecton is founder and CEO of Elite Building Services, a multimillion-dollar commercial cleaning and building maintenance company that serves clients nationally. She believes in treating her employees as well as her clients and lives by the motto, "If better is possible, good is not good enough." Elite Building Services is one of the largest women-owned businesses in the Mid-Atlantic region and has received awards from Smart CEO, DuPont, and EDIS, among others.

Cheryl is mother to two adult children and has two grandchildren. She lives on the East Coast with her husband.